My Mama Would Have Fought You

TINA MICHAEL

ISBN: 979-8-9959124-1-5

Dedication

For my mama, who fought for me when no one else would and taught me how to fight for more than myself.

For James, Eli, and Elise, you are the reason I will always get back up when I'm knocked down.

And for everyone who was told to sit down when they were meant to stand up, this story is for you.

Table of Contents

Maybe I was never meant to be the girl with the easy life.
Maybe I was meant to be the one who made it out with scars and stories.
The one who felt everything too much,
broke too many times to count but still showed up after walking through fire, carrying buckets for others.
Maybe my peace was never going to be quiet.
Maybe it was going to be purpose.
Some people get comfort. Some of us get called.

— *Tina Michael*

CHAPTER ONE

My Mama Would Have Fought You

I slipped out before the sun rose, just like I always do on Mother's Day. The streets were still asleep, and I liked it that way. No noise. No questions. Just me and the ache I carry. I parked where the grass is always a little too wet and the ground never feels steady under my feet. It does not matter. I have come here every year since she died, not because I think she is in the ground, but because I need a place to put my grief.

I stood over her grave and whispered the same words I always do. Thank you. I love you. I miss you. Then I added whatever my heart had not been brave enough to say out loud the rest of the year.

My mama is not here anymore, but somehow I still hear her. I still feel her. She shows up in the way I love my kids, in the way I walk through pain, in the way I give away pieces of myself the way she always did. Quietly. With no need to be seen.

She would have fought anybody who hurt me. And if she could not, she would have at least prayed for them real hard while making them a plate of food they did not deserve. That was her way. She had room in her heart for the loud ones, the broken ones, the kids who needed clean clothes, warm food, or someone to sit beside them for five quiet minutes. She mothered them all.

I still remember the first Mother's Day after I got pregnant with James, my oldest. My husband did not get me anything. Said I was not a mom yet. My mama did not agree. She showed up with a bright bouquet of neon flowers and that look in her eyes like she dared anyone to tell her I did not deserve it. I know she did not have much money that day, but she made sure I felt seen.

He might have been waiting for a baby to come out of me. She knew I became a mother the minute I started loving my baby boy.

That was just one moment. But there were so many.

And she did not do it because her life was easy. She carried trauma most people would not survive. But instead of turning cold, she turned toward people. She took her pain and used it as a blanket to wrap around everyone else. That was her version of healing. Loving people anyway.

I know if she could, she would give up Heaven to keep me from hurting. But since she cannot, she left her strength in me. I do not always feel it, but I know it is there.

At her grave, I asked God to help me love my kids the way she loved me. Fiercely. Unconditionally. With my whole heart, even on the days it is breaking.

Then I drove home before anyone noticed I was gone. I crept back inside and got under the covers like I had not just been crying beside a headstone. I did not want my kids to see my grief.

She would not want that either. She would want me to let myself be celebrated. She would want me to smile. Which is ironic, because, well... I cannot. That is not a metaphor. I literally cannot. But she would still want me to try.

And I did.

Even if I am not whole, I am still okay. Because she taught me how to be.

CHAPTER TWO

Laughed At, Looked Over, Loved Anyway

I do not remember the exact moment I realized I was different. I just remember the feeling. Like I was a puzzle piece that did not fit, but everyone else had silently agreed not to say it out loud. Some kids get their differences pointed out right away. Mine were written across my face whether I wanted them to be or not. I could hear it in the way people whispered when they thought I could not. I could feel it in the way grown-ups tilted their heads when they looked at me, like they were trying to smile without staring. Like they were trying to guess how much I knew.

And maybe the hardest part? I always knew. Even before I had the language for it. I was not what the world expected a little girl to look like. I was not the one people chose.

I used to think I had a dad. My stepdad was the only father I knew, and I believed he was mine. I had no reason to question it until the day they had to tell me the truth because of the adoption. It was not some big emotional sit-down. It was just something that had to be said.

That is when I found out about my biological father. And it was not just that he was gone. It was how he left. What he said. How cruel it really was.

I was told he denied I was his. That he said he did not make deformed babies. That my mom must have cheated on him because I was white and he was Mexican. My mom had to have an armed policeman stationed outside her hospital door. I did not even know what hate was at that age, but I felt what it did.

No matter how fiercely my mom loved me, no matter how hard she tried to protect me from all of it, that kind of rejection seeps in early. It lives in your bloodstream. It makes a home in the quiet places where you start to wonder what is wrong with you.

When I found out those things, I believed he was cruel. I believed what he said about me. I believed he did not want me, and I carried that truth like a scar no one could see.

I never imagined there might be more to the story. Not until decades later, when I met my sister. She told me he had been a good father to her. That was the first time I wondered if maybe he had changed. If maybe he was not a monster. Maybe he was just a man who walked away from one child and stayed for another.

I should have felt peace. But I felt jealousy. She got the version of him I always needed. She got the good dad, and I got the silence. The shame. The damage. And if he could want her, I figured the reason he did not want me had to be me.

But under all of that, I was truly grateful she had him. She deserved a good dad. I just wished I had one too.

My stepdad once told me that if I ever wanted to meet him, he would go with me. Not because he thought it would be sweet. He said it was because the man was dangerous. That was all I knew. So I never looked. But part of me still wondered if he ever looked for me.

The world made sure I never forgot I was different.

The first time someone called me retarded was on the playground in first grade. I remember exactly what I was wearing. I remember how loud the laughter was. I did not even understand the word, but I understood how it made me feel. Small. Ugly. Wrong.

I did not cry. I did not run. I just kept walking. That was the day I learned if I could make people laugh first, maybe they would not laugh at me.

But it was not just the words. The boy who called me that used to be in a circle with other boys at recess. They would push me down. I would get back up. They would push me down again. Over and over. I do not think the teachers even noticed. Or maybe they did and did nothing.

I told my stepdad once. I told him there were boys at recess who formed a circle around me and kept pushing me down. I would get back up, and they would push me down again. Over and over. He told me to just swing until I came into contact with something. Not to play. To fight back. I think he meant well. But I remember standing there with my fists closed, swinging at the air because that was the only way I knew to defend myself.

Spoiler: I did not hit anything. Except maybe the air's feelings.

That was around the same time I started looking to food for comfort. Not in a dramatic, movie-scene kind of way. Just in small, quiet moments. A snack after school when I felt alone. A second helping when I felt invisible. It became the one thing that did not push me down or push me away.

I had large-print books in class. Different ones than everyone else. Because I could not see well enough to read the regular ones. They were heavy and obvious and made me feel even more outside of things. But I carried them anyway.

School was not a place I looked forward to. It was a place I endured. Some kids had a favorite subject or friends that made things easier. I had a too-big backpack, a sharpened pencil, and a plan to make it through the day without crying.

I kept my head down. I learned who the safe teachers were. The ones who would not single me out with good intentions that felt like a spotlight. I hated attention. I also craved it.

It is strange to be both invisible and watched. I was not popular. But I was not ignored either. I lived in that space in between, where people notice you, just not in the way you want to be noticed.

There were kids who were mean on purpose, and others who said things that hurt without even realizing it. And once you have been laughed at for how you talk or walk or look, you learn to beat people to the joke.

That is where my humor came from.

I figured out how to say something first. If I could make the joke about myself, they could not use it against me. Laughing with them felt better than being laughed at.

And sometimes I really was funny. I had great timing. I knew how to land a line. People started to notice that. I was still different, but I was funny. And funny was useful.

It was my first currency.

Still, I wanted more than laughs.

I wanted to be liked. I wanted to be wanted. Not in the "she is so clever" kind of way. In the "she is the one I choose" kind of way.

There were things I could not do like other kids. I could not ride a bike. I could not run wild outside. My body had limits. But my mom never let that define me.

When other kids were playing, we were in the kitchen making cookies.

She let me pour the sugar even when it spilled everywhere. She let me crack the eggs even if the shell got in. She never made me feel like I was missing out. She just created a new kind of memory.

That kitchen became my safest place. It was warm, and it was ours. And without anyone meaning to, it taught me that food was part of feeling safe. I do not blame her. She was comforting me the best way she knew how. But in those bowls and mixing spoons, food quietly became more than just food.

She never let me use my disability as an excuse. She never let me settle. But she also never let me feel ashamed.

Doctors told her when I was born that I would never walk or talk. That she should put me in a home before she got too attached. But she never accepted that.

She looked that man in the face and basically said, "Watch me." And then she probably baked him a casserole anyway.

She fought for me like I was worth everything because to her, I was. When people said I would never walk, she held me up. When they said I would never talk, she would not stop talking to me. I was slow to do both, but I got there. Eventually, I did them at the same time and have not really stopped since.

When I was three years old, we passed one of those doctors in the hallway at the hospital. My mom looked at me and said, "Tell the doctor hi, Tina." And I did.

She put me in the Fort Worth State School for the Blind, but when she saw I was imitating the kids who were completely blind, running into walls, pretending I could not see at all, she said, "Nope. You do not need to be here."

When it came time for kindergarten, the public school would not take me. Too many needs. And private school was not an option. So I did not go.

But my mom made sure I was ready. She taught me everything I needed to know, and by the time first grade came around, I was not behind. I was prepared. She made sure of it.

In first grade, the school tried again to push me aside. But my mom stood up for me. She told them I was capable.

Just because my body was weak, didn't mean my mind was not sharp. They gave me a six-week trial.

I soared.

I was not just capable. I was one of the smart ones. Socially I struggled. But academically, I was strong. Because my mom made sure I was.

She never gave up on me. And she never let me give up on myself.

CHAPTER THREE

I Just Wanted to Be Chosen

I came home one night crying and telling my mama I was going to hell. I do not even know where the thought came from. I had not grown up in church. But somewhere, somehow, I had gotten the idea that something was deeply wrong with me and that when I died, I was not going where the good people go.

My mom did not try to explain it away. She did not tell me I was being silly or dramatic. She just picked up the phone and called a church. No appointment. No plan. Just a mother who loved her daughter and could not let her fall asleep that scared.

She told him what I had said that I was crying and could not be comforted. And even though it was the evening, he told her to come right then. He did not wait until morning or suggest we stop by later in the week. He said, "Come on."

That night, in a quiet church office, I met the first man who did not look at me with confusion or pity. Brother Bob did not flinch when he saw me. He did not search for the right words or stumble through the wrong ones. He just listened.

I told him what I was afraid of. That I was going to hell. That I did not know how to fix it. And he told me about Jesus, not like it was a Bible story, but like it was hope. Like someone had already done the saving and all I had to do was say yes.

I said yes that night.

It was the first time I believed there might be something good about me. Something worth redeeming.

That moment did not end when we left his office. Brother Bob became a steady presence in my life for years to come. He pastored the church that became my home, East Ridge Baptist. He baptized me. He taught me. And when I was grown and getting married, he officiated my wedding to John. He did not require the marriage counseling he normally did. He just said yes. Like he always had.

Even now, from afar, he is still in my life. Not always visible, but always there. Like a quiet thread God stitched into my story right when I needed it most.

Then there was my youth pastor. I wished he could have been my dad.

It was not a crush. It was deeper than that. I just wanted someone like him to belong to me. He made me feel safe and seen in a way most adults did not know how to do. He was kind without being fake, and funny without making me the punchline. When he talked to me, I did not feel like I had to shrink myself or prove anything. I could just be a kid.

I do not even know if he knew how much that meant to me.

When I heard his wife was pregnant, I remember feeling a twist in my chest I did not know how to name. I wanted to be that child. I wanted to be the one someone like him held and protected and loved without question. I wanted to belong to someone who looked at me the way a father looks at his little girl.

He showed up when I needed someone to. He did not just teach Bible lessons. He asked questions and actually listened to the answers. He made me feel like I mattered. Not because of what I could offer, or how I looked, but just because I was there.

And then he left.

He got another job, and I knew it had nothing to do with me. But it did not stop the ache that showed up in my chest when he was gone.

I know it was just a job change. But it felt personal. Every goodbye did back then. I was crushed.

There is a certain kind of grief that comes from someone leaving when they did not even know you were holding onto them. And I think that is when I started wishing harder for someone who would stay.

I think the first time I really believed someone might like me was in fourth grade. There was a boy in my class, the same one who had called me "retarded" on the playground back in first grade. The same one whose laugh still echoed in the back of my mind for years. But by fourth grade, something had changed. He started being kind. Not just polite but like he actually liked me. And when he asked me out, in whatever way fourth graders "go out," I said yes. Of course I did. I thought I had finally been picked.

For once, I was not just the funny one or the girl with the different books or the kid who sat out at recess. I was somebody's choice.

But it was not real.

I did not find out from him or even from my friend. Someone else in the class told me, loud enough for everyone to hear, that my friend had asked him to do it. That he was just doing it to be nice. And they all thought it was hilarious.

Turns out, being the punchline is not as fun when you do not know you are in a joke. I do not think my friend meant to hurt me. But she did. They all did.

It devastated me.

I carried that moment for years without realizing it. The kind of wound that hides behind every new friendship and crush. The kind that whispers, "They are only being nice because someone told them to." And you start to believe that maybe love is always a setup. A kindness wrapped in pity. A joke you did not know you were the punchline of.

Years later, when we were about twenty, the boy from my class apologized.

He was actually our waiter at Chili's while John and I were out eating, and there he was, standing at our table. He recognized me. I recognized him. And after all those years, he told me he was sorry.

Not just about that day in fourth grade, but about everything. The teasing. The pushing. The names. He looked me in the eye and said it like he meant it. He did not excuse it. He did not try to make it smaller. He just said sorry.

We kept in touch a little on Facebook after that. Nothing constant, but always kind. And in 2019, when I was in the hospital, he messaged me again. Told me how strong I was. That he had been following my story and admired me.

He did not have to say it. But he did. And that meant something.

He died not long after, from something he picked up while serving in Afghanistan. And even though we had not seen each other in years, I cried. Because some part of me had been holding that memory tight for so long, and now it was free.

Not everyone left.

Some people just stayed. No big entrance. No dramatic speeches. They just showed up and never stopped showing up.

That was Erin.

We met at church when I was fifteen. She was quiet. Not like me. I filled space with sound and jokes. She filled it with presence.

I made noise to be seen. She did not have to.

But something about her made me feel like I could just be. I did not have to perform. I did not have to explain.

She became my best friend without either of us really declaring it. She just started doing the things people who love you do.

She spent almost every weekend at my house. I would sleep in late, and she would be up early, just waiting for me to wake up. My mom kept a half gallon of Blue Bell in the freezer just for her because her mom never bought it at home. That was my mom's way, loving people quietly but fully.

We had a lot in common. We were both a little awkward, a little unsure of ourselves. We were soft around the edges, both physically and emotionally, but we felt safe with each other.

She used to drive me around even though she was only fifteen and did not have a license. I was sixteen and hated driving. But she was better at it than me, calmer somehow, like she was already grown in ways I was still figuring out.

When we had choir concerts, she helped me get into our formal varsity dresses before she even got herself ready. She brought me underwear once when I forgot to wear any to try on wedding dresses. No judgment. Just a bag and a smile.

She loaned me money so I could buy lingerie before I married John. Not because she thought it was a big deal, but because she knew I felt nervous and wanted to feel pretty.

And when my mom died, she sat in a room with me in total darkness. Not saying anything. Just being there when I could not move, when I could not think, when I could not believe the world kept turning without my mother in it.

She was there when all my babies were born. She has been there for every big moment since. Quiet. Steady. Herself.

She is my children's godmother. Not because of a title or a ceremony, but because there has never been a version of my life where she is not standing next to me when it matters most. If something ever happened to me, I would want her voice in their ears, her calm in their chaos, her steady love in their grief.

Erin is not the kind of person who takes up a lot of space. But she has filled some of the most important spaces in my life.

Then there was the first boy I ever loved. Of course, he did not love me back. Not in the way I wanted him to. But he was my friend, and that felt like something. Sometimes I thought maybe it was more. Sometimes I thought he looked at me differently. That maybe, just maybe, I had a chance.

He played guitar and sang beautifully. I would sit and listen like it was magic. He did not even have to try. His voice just carried something in it that made you want to lean closer. And I did. I always did.

We spent time together. Talked. Laughed. There was a softness in how he treated me that gave me hope. I remember once we went to Taco Delight. just the two of us. I wanted to believe it was a date. I told myself it might be. I held onto that maybe like it could turn into something real.

I was always holding onto maybes. They felt safer than nos.

But then my Sweet 16 happened.

We had the party at the church, because that is where I lived half my life. Youth events, worship nights, weekends. That was my space. My safe place.

And that night, he started dating someone else.

I do not remember what they said or how it happened. I just remember standing in the middle of my own party and feeling invisible. Like I was just the backdrop for someone else's love story.

They got married not long after. He was not even out of high school yet. I think he had just turned eighteen.

They divorced eventually. He has been married two more times since then. All of them ended.

Sometimes I thank God for unanswered prayers.

But back then, it destroyed me. I told myself maybe he did like me, just not enough. Maybe he was embarrassed to be seen with someone like me. Maybe my face was what got in the way. Or my body. Or both.

I will never know for sure.

All I knew was that I had let myself believe I could be wanted. And when that belief shattered, it cut deep.

Then there was a friend of mine, the kind who hung around even when things got weird. He took me to junior prom. I remember wondering if my mom had asked him to. Especially since we took her brand-new Dodge Ram truck, and he called her "Mama Bear" because they really were close.

He loved my mom. Everyone did. But the way he talked to her had something more to it, like she gave him the same safety she gave me.

My mom bought me three prom dresses. I tried them on at home, twirling around the living room like a girl in a movie, hoping I looked beautiful, even if no one said it. My date did not say much while I modeled them. But another friend of his was there. He watched closely. He told me I looked beautiful in the black one. And sometimes I think he actually meant it. I ended up wearing the blue.

I wished I had the courage to believe someone like him might have actually liked me. But I did not. I could not see it. Not then.

My prom date and I were never romantic. He felt like a brother more than anything else. He never acted ashamed of me, and I clung to that. It was rare to have a friendship that felt simple and safe.

But then, right after junior year ended, everything shifted.

My parents went to Vegas and left me home alone for the first time in my life. A whole week. My mom had him stay to keep an eye on me. Maybe she trusted me. Or maybe she thought no boy would ever want me. Either way, she was wrong.

We were just horseplaying one night, bouncing around like kids. I fell on the bed, and he fell on top of me.

That was it. That was the moment everything changed. I had never even been kissed before. And that night, I lost my virginity without ever being kissed. I remember making him go out to his truck to get a condom. I do not know why. Maybe I thought it would make it feel like a decision, something with purpose instead of something we stumbled into. Maybe I wanted to feel like it counted.

But afterward, he just went back to his girlfriend. And nothing ever really changed. It was not how I wanted my first time to be. It was not soft or special. It just was.

He came to my mom's funeral. He did not say much. He just stood there. But it mattered to me that he came. That even after everything, even after so many years and so much silence, he showed up when it really counted.

My mom had a lot of kids and teenagers who came to her over the years. She was everyone's mom. The one who made you feel safe without asking questions. The one who always had something in the fridge and time to listen.

My cousin lived with us for a while when she was a baby. Her mom was going through a divorce, and my mom stepped in without blinking.

Josh, my cousin, my mom's brother's son, was always like my brother. Even when my Mamaw was alive, my mom took care of him just like she did me. We only lived five minutes apart, so he was part of our everyday life. When my Mamaw died when we were sixteen, and then his dad died too, Josh came to live with us. But truthfully, nothing really changed. He had always belonged there.

Then there was another friend of mine.

We were going into seventh or eighth grade, I believe, when CPS took her from her home because her stepdad hit her. My mom did not hesitate. She opened our door to her like it was the most natural thing in the world. No judgment. No red tape. Just love.

That was who she was. A soft place to land, no matter where you were falling from. And I think that is why my prom date came to her funeral. Because she was his Mama Bear too.

Maybe that is all some people are meant to do in your life. Not stay. Just show up once more when it matters most.

CHAPTER FOUR

I Became Who They'd Stay For

I had spent so much of my life trying to be chosen that I forgot I was allowed to choose myself. Growing up, I looked for mirrors in other people. I wanted someone to reflect back to me that I was beautiful. That I was wanted. That I was enough.

And when I did not find that in the world around me, I tried to become someone people would pick.

I was funny. I was giving. I worked hard to be the kind of girl who made it easy for people to love her.

I used to spend hours helping people write their papers or edit their speeches, even when I had my own to finish. I would show up with coffee, offer to drive someone home, sit in someone's room and listen for hours when they were going through it. I was not doing it just to be kind. I think I just hoped that if I made myself helpful enough, needed enough, no one would forget me.

But when the laughter faded and the quiet set in, I realized I was not just trying to be loved. I was trying to earn my place in rooms that never saw me to begin with.

Adulthood did not fix that. It just gave me more places to disappear. More people to lose myself in. More ways to convince myself that if I was just good enough, quiet enough, useful enough, someone would stay.

But somewhere in the middle of trying to belong to everyone else, I started learning what it might mean to belong to myself.

I wish I could say I figured it all out right away. That once I left home and started college, I suddenly knew my worth and walked in it. But that would be a lie.

I went to Dallas Baptist University. A Christian school. A place where purity was preached and grace was always on the sign out front. But I did not feel pure. And I did not feel graceful. I just felt alone.

My face did not look like the other girls' faces. It never had. I could not smile. I could not pose for a picture and look effortlessly beautiful. And my body? It never looked the way I was told it should. Not by TV. Not by boys. Not even by the church.

And when you grow up starving for love, you start mistaking crumbs for a feast.

So I looked for connection the only way I knew how. In bodies. In beds. In moments that felt like they might mean something even when they did not.

One guy I was friends with took me to see Titanic at the drive-in. But we did not watch the movie. I knew then, and still now, almost thirty years later, that I was expected to take that night to my grave. He would be embarrassed if anyone found out. That kind of closeness never came with care. It came with shame and silence.

There were more men than I ever imagined I would let close to me. More than I could count. More than I care to remember.

And honestly? I was surprised anyone ever wanted to. I had spent so long believing no one would. That no man would ever see me and still want to touch me. I carried so much shame about my face, about my body, about not looking like the girls I saw in magazines or even just walking through the mall. So when someone did want me, even for a night, I let myself believe maybe that was the only kind of love I would ever get.

That is not something I say for shock or shame. It is just the truth.

Because I was not reckless. I was lonely. I was not wild. I was tired of feeling unwanted. My face did not look like the other girls'. I could not smile the way they did. My body never looked like the ones that got picked first. I was always too much or not enough.

Too different. Too visible and yet unseen.

So I gave myself away in pieces. Not because I did not care, but because I cared too much. I kept hoping someone would see past the outside and stay for the inside. But they never did.

I went to a Christian college. I knew the words they used for girls like me, so I stayed quiet. I wore the right shirts. I smiled as best I could. I raised my hands in worship and wondered if God was disappointed in me.

But underneath all the hymns and hopes was a girl who was breaking apart quietly. A girl who just wanted someone, anyone, to see her and not walk away.

They did not stay. Until I met John.

I had started to believe love was not something that happened to girls like me. At best, I thought maybe I would get someone who tolerated me. Someone who stayed because they were too polite to leave. But John did not tolerate me. He saw me. He did not flinch or fidget when I talked about things that scared me. He leaned in. He laughed. He listened. And he loved me without making me earn it.

He was never ashamed to be seen with me in daylight. He held my hand in public. He kissed me in front of people. Not like he was showing off. Like he was proud.

John used to tell me he did not even notice my facial paralysis until I pointed it out. I did not believe him at first. How could he not? It had always felt like the first thing everyone else saw. But he meant it. He said he saw me. Not what did not move, but what did. My eyes. My heart. My fire.

I did not have a name for my condition back then. Not yet. I would not get that diagnosis until much later. After a tumor. After heartbreak. After everything. I had lived more than three decades believing I was just different in a way no one else understood. I did not know there were others like me. I did not know I belonged somewhere.

But John chose me anyway.

And when he asked me to marry him, he did it in a way I will never forget. He left a trail of love letters through the house, each one guiding me to the next. I will never forget how it felt to read them, one by one, until I got to the last one waiting just outside the bedroom door.

Tina,
When you come into this door, you're coming into my life forever.
My threshold is now OUR threshold. This is the last one you'll ever have to cross alone. From now on we cross them together. From now on we face everything together.
There are so many aspects of my love for you, that I don't want to describe them all in one note. Please check the dining room table, and then the fridge, and then the bedroom door for others.

Yours forever,
John

p.s. I'm in the bedroom right now, and I have something for you☺
But read the notes first please.

Transcription

Tina,

When you come into this door, you are coming into my life forever. My threshold is now OUR threshold. This is the last one you will ever have to cross alone. From now on we cross them together. From now on we face everything together.

There are so many aspects of my love for you that I do not want to describe them all in one note. Please check the dining room table, and then the fridge, and then the bedroom door for others.

Yours forever, John

P.S. I am in the bedroom right now, and I have something for you. But read the notes first please.

My Baby,
I'm leaving a note on the table because it symbolizes how we're family now. We'll eat together, and laugh together, and love together, and sometimes even fight together. Because that's what families do.
Right now we're a small family with only two chairs. But as we grow in love, and grow in maturity, and grow in faith in one another, the number of chairs will grow too. More mouths to feed, and more hearts to share. We'll always have enough love. No matter how big the table eventually becomes.

With all my love,
John

Transcription

My Baby,

I am leaving a note on the table because it symbolizes how we are family now. We will eat together, and laugh together, and love together, and sometimes even fight together. Because that is what families do.

Right now we are a small family with only two chairs. But as we grow in love, and grow in maturity, and grow in faith in one another, the number of chairs will grow too. More mouths to feed, and more hearts to share. We will always have enough love. No matter how big the table eventually becomes.

With all my love, John

My Dear,
Just like we get ingredients from the fridge to make our meals, I'm thankful that you and I had the right ingredients to make our love last. With a little bit of understanding, more than just a pinch of patience, and more devotion than anyone could ever measure, we've become one.
Whoever the chef is, give him my compliments. Because what we have turned out better than I ever would have hoped for.

I love you dearly,
John

Transcription

My Dear,

Just like we get ingredients from the fridge to make our meals, I am thankful that you and I had the right ingredients to make our love last. With a little bit of understanding, more than just a pinch of patience, and more devotion than anyone could ever measure, we have become one.

Whoever the chef is, give him my compliments. Because what we have turned out better than I ever would have hoped for.

I love you dearly, John

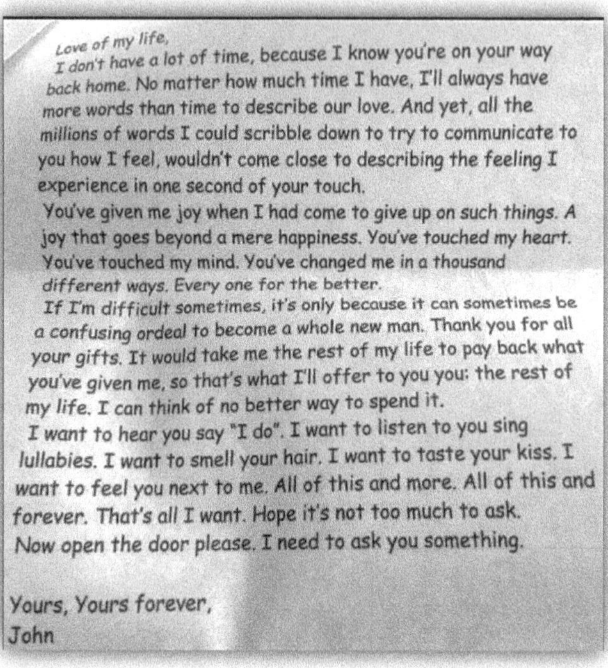

Love of my life,
I don't have a lot of time, because I know you're on your way back home. No matter how much time I have, I'll always have more words than time to describe our love. And yet, all the millions of words I could scribble down to try to communicate to you how I feel, wouldn't come close to describing the feeling I experience in one second of your touch.
You've given me joy when I had come to give up on such things. A joy that goes beyond a mere happiness. You've touched my heart. You've touched my mind. You've changed me in a thousand different ways. Every one for the better.
If I'm difficult sometimes, it's only because it can sometimes be a confusing ordeal to become a whole new man. Thank you for all your gifts. It would take me the rest of my life to pay back what you've given me, so that's what I'll offer to you you: the rest of my life. I can think of no better way to spend it.
I want to hear you say "I do". I want to listen to you sing lullabies. I want to smell your hair. I want to taste your kiss. I want to feel you next to me. All of this and more. All of this and forever. That's all I want. Hope it's not too much to ask.
Now open the door please. I need to ask you something.

Yours, Yours forever,
John

Transcription

Love of my life,

I do not have a lot of time, because I know you are on your way back home. No matter how much time I have, I will always have more words than time to describe our love.

And yet, all the millions of words I could scribble down to try to communicate to you how I feel would not come close to describing the feeling I experience in one second of your touch.

You have given me joy when I had come to give up on such things. A joy that goes beyond a mere happiness. You have touched my heart. You have touched my mind. You have changed me in a thousand different ways. Every one for the better.

If I am difficult sometimes, it is only because it can sometimes be a confusing ordeal to become a whole new man. Thank you for all your gifts. It would take me the rest of my life to pay back what you have given me, so that is what I will offer to you: the rest of my life. I can think of no better way to spend it.

I want to hear you say I do. I want to listen to you sing lullabies. I want to smell your hair. I want to taste your kiss. I want to feel you next to me. All of this and more. All of this and forever. That is all I want. Hope it is not too much to ask.

Now open the door please. I need to ask you something.

Yours forever, John

That was the moment. The day I realized someone saw all of me. Past the paralysis. Past the pain. Past the years of believing I was unworthy. And still wanted to build a life with me.

And I said yes.

We got engaged in November of 1999 and married on March 18, 2000. Less than five months between the question and the commitment, and not a single moment of doubt in between.

That is not to say it was perfect. No marriage is. But I went into it knowing that for the first time in my life, I was not chasing love. I was walking with it. I was choosing it right back.

John was not just the first man to stay. He was the first one who really saw me, even the parts of me I tried to hide. And he loved me anyway. He still does.

Our life together started with promises scribbled on notes, and it quickly turned into real life. Messy. Beautiful. Full of growing pains and grace.

We lost a baby in July of 2000. I had a miscarriage, and it broke something in me I did not even know could break. But John held me through it. He did not have the words, but he stayed. And sometimes staying is the loudest love language of all.

Four years later, James was born. James Dixon Michael. September 5, 2004.

There was no Instagram back then. No perfectly posed hospital photos or curated captions. Just the raw, sacred reality of becoming a mother.

I was swollen and exhausted, and I could not smile with my face, but my eyes said everything. That was one of the most alive moments of my life.

And my mom lit up when she held him. Her face softened in a way I had not seen in a long time. She glowed with pride and joy.

She used to call him Boogie, because he stayed up and kept us up boogieing all night long.

He was her pride and joy, even though I think deep down, she was already starting to drown in herself.

We had just moved to Granbury, two minutes from her house, when I was eight months pregnant. Before that, we were in Arlington. I am so thankful we got those two years close to her. I did not know it at the time, but they would be our last.

She died almost two months after James turned two.

I do not know where her death belongs in this story yet. Maybe it belongs in every part. Because she has never really left me.

But in that moment, holding my son, watching her hold him, I felt something sacred. Like the love that raised me was stretching forward into the next generation. And I was the bridge.

That bridge kept stretching. On October 12, 2012, I gave birth to twins, Elijah Evan and Elise Elliott. We went from a family of three to a family of five overnight.

Everything doubled. The diapers, the feedings, the exhaustion, the love. It was beautiful and brutal all at once. I remember holding one baby while reaching for the other, already wondering how I was going to do it all.

I was not even sure I could hold them both without dropping one.

And in that moment, I made them a promise, a promise that I would never drop them. I knew I might trip. I knew I might even fall, but I also knew I would never allow either of them to hit the ground.

James had felt easy in comparison. This was different. Louder. Harder. Everything at once.

Even then, I could see pieces of who they were going to be.

Eli, steady and determined, the kind who would get frustrated but never quit.

Elise, bold and fearless, already carrying a fire that was not going to be quiet.

They were going to stretch me in ways I did not understand yet.

But I looked at their faces — his so calm, hers already full of fire — and I knew I would find a way. I always had.

My motherhood has never looked perfect. But it has always been fierce. And maybe that is what she passed down to me, more than anything. That relentless kind of love. The kind that stretches across generations and still shows up, even when you are tired, even when you are unsure, even when you are breaking a little inside.

And somewhere in the middle of that bridge, I started to realize I do not have to hide my thoughts to be loved.

I do not have to silence my truth to make someone else feel safe.

I used to think I embarrassed people just by existing too loudly, dreaming too big, or feeling too deeply.

But I have lived too long in that quiet. And I am done apologizing for my mind, my fire, or my story. My thoughts are not too much. They are finally mine.

CHAPTER FIVE

I Didn't Know It Was Goodbye

November 17th, 2006. Thirteen days after her forty-eighth birthday. She had Burger King for lunch that day. That was unusual. She had borrowed my car to go to the doctor, and she called to ask if she could use the change in the cup holder to grab food. I told her yes, even though part of me was frustrated. I thought she went to the doctor too much. She did not have insurance. It felt wasteful. My parents only had one working car. We were moving into our new house the next day. I had asked her earlier that week to come see it. She said she would wait until we were settled in.

I thought she was just being lazy again.

She didn't say much about her appointment when she got back. My dad had just gotten paid, so for dinner she picked minestrone soup from Pastafina, her favorite. She seemed okay. John and I had grabbed Jack in the Box. James had just turned two in September, and we were all staying at her house until the move.

She adored James. He was the light of her world. She called him Boogie because he liked to stay up and boogie all night long.

Before bed, she bent down and kissed him goodnight. He turned his head away like toddlers do, but it didn't bother her. She smiled and said, "I love you, Boogie," and walked down the hall to her room. That was the last thing she ever said.

If I had known it would be, I would've made him kiss her back. I would've kissed her too. I would've told her she was everything good in my life and I didn't know how to live without her.

But I didn't know. And I didn't say any of it.

Later that night, John and I made microwave burritos around midnight. I can't remember for sure if I heard her snore after that. Maybe I only thought I did. Her snoring used to shake the walls.

Sometimes it scared me. Sometimes it comforted me. She was supposed to wear a CPAP but rarely did. That night I think I heard it. But maybe she was already gone.

We were asleep on the couch when I heard it.

A crash. Then shouting. Then pounding footsteps.

The front door slammed open with such force it shook the house. For a second, I thought we were being robbed. The paramedics stormed past us like we weren't even there. My dad had called 911 but in his panic forgot to unlock the door. So they broke it in. They didn't stop. Didn't knock. Didn't say a word. Just rushed toward her room like they already knew it was too late.

Someone said, "She's gone." I ran.

I didn't wait for permission. I didn't care who tried to stop me. I shoved my way past uniforms and gear and fear and dropped to the floor beside her.

She was cold. And blue. And already stiff. But I held her anyway.

I cradled her like she had cradled me so many times. My arms were shaking. My voice broke. I begged God to give her back. I screamed for Him not to do this. I told Him to take me instead. I called out every verse I had ever believed in. I cried into her nightgown and kissed her hair and sobbed into the crook of her neck like a child.

Her silky nightgown clung to my arms. My tears soaked her hair. Her body was still. But I stayed there anyway.

I asked Him to raise her like Lazarus.

I kept thinking if I just held her tighter, cried louder, prayed harder, He would change His mind. But He didn't.

And I was so angry.

I wasn't ready to let go. I wasn't ready to hear silence where her voice should be. I wasn't ready to be motherless. I didn't care what reason He had. I didn't care how peaceful they said it was. I wanted her back. I needed her back. And He didn't give her to me.

But somewhere in the wreckage of that moment, I pictured her in glory.

I imagined her healed. Whole. No more pain. No more pretending to be okay when her body screamed otherwise. And that hurt in a different way. Because I knew without a doubt that she would have traded every bit of Heaven's glory to stay here with me. Even in her pain. Even if it cost her everything.

Because that's who she was.

She always put me before herself. Always.

The coroner said it was a heart attack. That she had been gone for hours. I will never know if that's true. She had been taking pain pills for years. Her body hurt all the time. I never thought she took too many. She wasn't like that. But maybe she forgot she had already taken some.

Maybe the pain got too loud and she needed more than they told her was safe. Maybe it was an accident. Maybe it wasn't the pills at all.

Maybe her body just gave up before the rest of us were ready to let go. I don't know.

Her PCP called afterward and told me he hadn't prescribed her many. But was he covering himself? Was she seeing other doctors? Doctor shopping was common back then. I didn't know to ask those questions. I wish I had.

I think my dad wondered too. He hid her pillbox from the paramedics. Maybe he didn't want them jumping to conclusions. Maybe he already had.

No autopsy was performed. The county only allotted a limited number each year and reserved them for suspected foul play. That was the policy. And just like that, every question we had was left unanswered.

The funeral is mostly a blur.

But I remember asking people to share stories about her. And they did. Most people in my situation wouldn't have spoken under those circumstances. But I did. I had to. I don't remember much of what I said. I just remember knowing I had to say something. Because silence didn't protect her. And it wouldn't protect me either.

She didn't have life insurance. I was twenty-seven with a toddler and a husband in an entry-level job. I didn't have the money to bury her. I felt like a failure. But my mamaw's siblings stepped in. My Aunt Margaret and her husband Jack, Uncle Dan and his wife Donnie, and Uncle John and his wife Nelda paid for the funeral. Aunt Margaret sat with me in the funeral director's office and told me it wasn't my responsibility to carry that weight. She still let me make every decision. I tried to pay her back years later, but she wouldn't take it. She said the others wouldn't either. That's just what families do.

Aunt Margaret was there when the twins were born. She helped take care of them when I was sick. Bought formula and diapers. Cleaned my house even though she had a housekeeper of her own. She was boujee like that. Really boujee. She was there when they took out my tumor. I didn't go see her as much as I should have once the twins got older. She passed away in 2024 at ninety-two.

My Aunt Nana stayed close too. She was my mamaw's youngest sister and had been close to my mom since she was a teenager. She has stayed close to me even now. She always reminds me that I was never alone.

After the funeral, the doctor put me on anxiety meds. John had to go back to work. He worked nights and slept during the day. I was alone. I would send James to the sitter and sit on the couch in the quiet. And the phone never rang. There were no casseroles. No cards. No one stopped by. I had lost the person who made the world make sense, and all I heard in response was silence.

I remember thinking I could walk onto the freeway and not even care if a car hit me. That's when I stopped taking the pills.

Because I needed to feel it. She deserved to be mourned. And James deserved a mom who cared.

In the days that followed, I would call her phone just to hear her voicemail. I didn't even think to record it. Technology wasn't what it is now. The day AT&T deleted her greeting, it felt like she died all over again.

We moved from Granbury back to Arlington. I couldn't drive past her house. We had a tiny apartment, but it didn't matter. I kept the CD from her funeral in my car stereo for more than three years. Every time I was alone, I would play it and cry.

One day, I came outside to go to work, and my stereo was gone. Someone had stolen it. Just the cheap factory unit. But they took the CD too. I was furious. Then I prayed. Maybe they listened to it. Maybe they needed it. Maybe my mama touched someone through it. Even from heaven.

She always told me, when you're struggling, the best thing you can do is take your focus off yourself and do something to help someone else. And she meant it.

One of the only times in her life that she had extra money, she bought a statue for her church. A beautiful sculpture of the Bride of Christ, arms raised to heaven, her face glowing with devotion.

She donated it without fanfare. She didn't need recognition. She just wanted to give something beautiful back to the God she loved. She struggled her whole life, but she still believed in giving.

She never got to meet Eli and Elise.

She would have adored them. She would have laughed at Elise's sass and marveled at Eli's quiet strength. She would have loved them the way she loved James, with her whole being. I grieve that as much as I grieve losing her.

James was only two. For weeks after she died, every time we would drive near Walmart, he would ask, "Is Nanny there?" The funeral home was just across the street, and in his little mind, that was where she lived now. It was sweet. And it was unbearable.

She didn't get to grow old.

She didn't get to sit on a front porch, drink sweet tea, and spoil her grandbabies. She didn't get to be the woman I called when motherhood felt like too much. She didn't get to be here. And I didn't get to learn how to live without her.

Now I'm trying to teach my kids how to do what I never could.

How to keep going if something happens to me. How to survive a loss like that. I don't even know how to say it out loud. Just that I don't want them to feel what I felt. But every time I try to prepare them, it breaks something open in me. Because all I wanted was my mama. And she didn't leave me instructions. She left me love. But no road map.

I've made it almost twenty years. And I still don't know how.

People think time softens grief. It doesn't. It just teaches you how to carry it without screaming. I've learned how to smile in pictures even though I physically can't. I've raised babies she never held. I've celebrated birthdays, holidays, and milestones without her. I've gone through things that should have broken me. And somehow the world just kept turning.

But I've felt every spin.

Every year that took me farther from the sound of her voice. I still need her.

I needed her when my daughter first said Mama. I needed her when I sat in dark rooms trying to feel okay again. I needed her when I wasn't sure if I was going to make it.

And I need her still.

That part has never changed.

Sometimes when someone's elderly parent dies, a part of me shuts down. I hate that about myself. But I understand it. They had decades. I had a door kicked in and a body gone cold. I didn't just lose my mother. I lost decades. And I'm still angry about that.

People always say she was lucky. That she didn't suffer. That she died in her sleep. But that never brought me comfort. I don't want that for myself. When I die, I want to be awake. I want to know it's coming. Even if it hurts. Even if there's pain. Because being able to say goodbye matters more than comfort.

I never told people how much I hated the pills. How I hated that she needed them just to get through the day. How I hated that the world handed her pain and expected her to be fine. How I hated that the medicine might have taken her, even if she never meant for it to.

But I'm saying it now.

Because grief isn't always graceful. Sometimes it's bitter. Sometimes it's jealous. Sometimes it shows up dressed like shame.

I don't like that part of me. But I understand it. Because she wasn't just my mother.

She was my safe place. My reason. My home. The one who always made the world make sense.

She sang loudly in church even though she couldn't carry a tune. When I would cringe, she would say, "I'm making a joyful noise to the Lord." She really believed that. I think maybe He did too.

She wasn't perfect. But she was real. And she was mine.

She was more than how she died. More than what she took. More than what she left behind.

She was loud and loving and soft and strong. She gave more than she had. She kept showing up for everyone but herself.

She was my mama.

And I didn't know it was goodbye.

I hated those pills.

Not just because they might have taken her.

But because they were a symbol of everything she was forced to carry alone.

She was in pain for so long that needing them became her normal.

And no one ever stopped to ask what kind of world demands that a woman stay strong and silent while she suffers.

No one offered her a way out that didn't come with side effects or shame. So she took what she had to take. And I loved her for surviving it.

But I still hated the medicine. I hated what it represented. And I always will.

She didn't leave a road map.

She left fight.

She left fierce love. She left me.

And every time I stand when the world tells me to sit,
every time I choose tenderness when anger would be easier,
every time I stay soft, stay kind, stay here,
it's because she taught me how.

She was the gospel of a girl the world tried to break. And I am the woman her love refused to leave broken.

CHAPTER SIX

She Gave Me What She Never Got

She died on November 18, 2006. Her birthday had been just two weeks earlier, November 5. She turned 48 that year. I wanted to throw her a surprise party. I thought about it, dreamed about it, even started to plan it in my head. But I never did. And I have carried that regret ever since.

She was never celebrated the way she should have been. I do not even know if she ever had a real birthday party. But she made sure I had one every single year, no matter how much pain she was in or how little money we had. She made joy out of nothing.

She created magic on a dime. And still, I left her last birthday quiet and unmarked, because I did not know it would be her last.

Twelve years later, I was standing in the checkout line at Albertsons when I saw a woman in front of me put back a birthday cake. She could not afford it. She said it was for her mother, whose

70th birthday was that day. I quietly told the cashier to put the cake on my bill and sneak it into her basket without saying anything.

She walked away, but then came rushing back in a panic to tell the cashier she had not paid for the cake. That is when he told her someone already had. She got tears in her eyes and told me she was just trying to make dinner special for her mom.

I made it to my car before I lost it. I sat there and cried for twenty minutes. Because I should have given my mom a cake. I should have made her birthday feel special. But I did not. Not because I did not want to, because I did not know it would be her last.

But maybe I did give her a cake after all. Not on her birthday, not when it mattered most, but later, when another mother needed it. I gave her a cake in heaven. Because she would have gladly given her own cake away here on earth. That is who she was.

She had become morbidly obese by then. She had always carried extra weight, but in those final years, it consumed her. She stopped going to church. She started pulling away from people. She stayed in bed more than she did not. I used to think she just needed to lose some weight and get up and try harder. I thought she was being dramatic. I even thought she was a hypochondriac sometimes. I did not understand.

But no matter how bad it got, she still got out of bed to make dinner. She could sleep through the day, miss appointments, ignore the phone, but when it came time for supper, she was up. Usually just for my dad once I was grown, but also for anyone else who might be there. And there was always someone. A friend. A neighbor. Someone who needed a plate and a place to sit. She made sure they had both.

Once, we were at a women's church retreat and she started acting strange. Her movements were slow. She seemed confused, like she could not quite focus. I was humiliated. I thought she was high. Or faking. I thought she just wanted attention.

But some of the women around us were worried. They said something was not right and convinced her to go to the hospital. We got her there, and it turned out it was not drugs.

It was not drama. She was in congestive heart failure. Her oxygen levels were dangerously low.

Even after the doctor told me what was really happening, I still doubted her. I still thought she might be exaggerating. I look back on that now and feel sick with shame. I was so sure I knew what was going on. But I had no idea what she was carrying.

And maybe that was part of the problem. My parents were poor. My mom did not have a car of her own. Toward the end of her life, they had one vehicle between them, and even that one did not always run. She had no insurance and therefore practically no healthcare. My dad always had the car at work. So even if she wanted help, she would have had no way to get there. I know she felt trapped. I would feel trapped too if I could not come and go as I pleased. If I had to ask permission or wait around just to go see a doctor. Just to breathe.

I wish she had what I have now. I may not have good health, but I have good healthcare. I am never denied the treatment I need because of money. And that is because of John. He makes sure I am covered. He makes sure I get what I need. She never had that. She deserved it.

And if she were here, she would say she was glad I had it, even if it meant she never did. But that is not the point. We both deserved it. We both should have had it.

I did not see it for what it really was. Grief. Addiction. Trauma. Exhaustion. The weight of everything she had never said out loud.

She was abused as a child. And not just emotionally. There was sexual abuse. Physical abuse. Neglect. Her stepmother was cruel in ways most people never talk about. She had to cook for her brothers and was not allowed to eat until they were finished. And sometimes, there was not anything left.

She never said much about it, but when she did, her voice got small. Like she was still that little girl in the kitchen, waiting for scraps. Like speaking it out loud might make it real again.

Her own mother left her behind when she divorced her dad. And yet, decades later, my mama took care of that same mother when she was dying of bone cancer. She fed her. She bathed her. She sat with her through the end. And she did it without bitterness.

Without ever throwing the past in her face. That is just who she was.

She made dinner every Wednesday for the entire church congregation for years. It was her joy. Her offering. And when Sunday came around, she would sit in the pew and sing off-key as loud as she could. I used to be embarrassed by it. I would squirm in my seat, wishing she would lower her voice. But now I know. It was a joyful noise. Her praise was real and unashamed.

Still, there were things I was ashamed of back then. Like how my clothes and hair always smelled like smoke. We did not have much, and we lived in whatever we could afford. I did not realize at the time that she was doing the best she could with what she had. I just wanted to blend in. I just did not want to be different anymore.

I think the addiction started after Mamaw died. My mom took care of her when no one else could or would. She held onto so much hurt for so long. When Mamaw was gone, I think a part of her gave up. And she started reaching for whatever would numb the ache.

My mama was a good, Jesus-fearing woman.

She was also addicted to opioids. She smoked cigarettes. She turned to food when the pain got too loud. And for a long time, I did not understand why she could not stop. Why she stayed in bed. Why she let herself disappear.

But now I know. Addiction does not make you bad. It makes you human. And sometimes, the strongest people are the ones who carry their pain the quietest.

She had a hard life. A life full of struggle and survival. And I wish more than anything she had gotten to live the kind of life she helped me reach.

Because that is the truth. She helped me get here. Her sacrifices. Her fight. Her faith in me. It paved the road I walk now.

I used to sit at the edge of the kitchen and just watch her cook. Spanish rice was her signature. I must have seen her make it a hundred times, but I never joined in. Never chopped. Never stirred. I think I assumed she would always be there to do it.

When she died, all I wanted was to taste that rice again. I tried over and over, but it never came out quite right. Not for almost twenty years. I did not realize how much I had taken for granted. How much knowledge lives in the hands of the people we love until they are not there to show us anymore.

When I was little, doctors and educators told her to put me in a home. Told her not to get too attached. Told her I would never walk, never talk, never have a real life. Later, when it came time to go to school, they tried to put me in a class meant for students with intellectual disabilities. That is the more respectful term now. But back then, it was just the slow class.

They said I would not keep up. That I did not belong in a regular classroom. But she did not listen. She fought. She said, her mind works just fine. They gave her six weeks to prove it. I thrived. And I have been thriving ever since, because she believed in me when no one else did.

And here is what I understand now as a grown woman. You adapt to the environment you are given. If she had listened to them, if she had put me in that class or in a facility, I would have become what they expected. I would have shrunk to fit their limits.

But she did not let them decide who I was. She made sure I had the chance to become me.

She loved James so much. From the moment he was born, she doted on him like he hung the moon. He reminded her of me. She used to hold his face in her hands the way she did mine, whispering, "You are so special." I know she meant it.

But toward the end, I could not trust her to watch him while I worked. I did not know how bad things were yet. I had not put all the pieces together. But I could feel something was off. She was tired all the time. She forgot things. Her body moved slower. It broke my heart to make that decision. I never told her outright, but I started making other arrangements. I carried guilt about that for years. Still do.

She never got to meet Eli or Elise. They were born after she was gone. But sometimes James looks so much like her it knocks the wind out of me. Elise makes some of her same expressions, especially when she is annoyed.

She would have loved them fiercely. And they would have loved her right back. She would have been at every single one of James's little league games.

I do not even have to imagine it. I know it. She would have parked herself right behind the backstop, hollering louder than anyone, probably embarrassing him in the best way. The whole team would have called her Mama Bear, just like my old friend from prom did. That was her role. Protector. Loudest cheerleader. Heart of the bench.

She and my stepdad were team mom and coach when they did not even really have a kid on the team, just Josh. But that did not matter. If you were hers, she showed up.

She would have said James got his Beltre-like flexibility from her side of the family, especially when he was catching behind the plate or stretching for a play at first. And when he hit that grand slam, she would have jumped out of her seat and screamed until she was hoarse. I can see it. I can hear it. Because that is exactly who she was.

Eli would have amazed her.

His brilliance. His quiet strength. The way his mind works like a maze of strategy and compassion. She would have told every single person that her grandson plays chess like a champion. She would have said he got his smarts from her side of the family, just like she would have said James got his athleticism from her too. She would have bragged about Eli to anyone who would listen, and even to those who did not.

She would have seen how special he is. And she would have made sure he knew it too.

And Elise. She would have had her wrapped around her finger.

She has that same fire. The same stubborn streak. The same steel in her eyes when she digs in her heels. If I ever tried to get onto her, my mama would have stepped right in and said, "She is mine. I am your mama, and what I say goes." Then she would have slipped Elise something sweet, told me to hush, and whispered, "Do not tell your mom."

She would not have let me win a single argument. I would have rolled my eyes and loved her for it anyway.

My mama told me once that my biological father abused her. It was not just hitting. It was controlling. Degrading. Dehumanizing. She told me she did not love herself enough to leave him at first. But she loved me enough to get out. That was her turning point. Not her pain, but my safety. She left for me.

I later learned that my sister had a different experience with him. That he found Jesus. That he changed. I did not know that until after she died. But I think my mama would have been glad to hear it. She would have been proud of him. She would have wanted him in heaven too.

My mama was a good, Jesus-fearing woman. Not because she was perfect. Not because she had it easy. But because she never let go of God, even when the rest of the world let go of her.

Her life was messy. Complicated. Flawed. But it was also brave and faithful and full of relentless love.

This is her testimony. Not the addiction. Not the weight. Not the cigarettes. This. The life she gave to me, even when hers was falling apart. The strength she passed down, even when she did not know she had any left. The way she loved me, even when she could not love herself. She did not get the life she deserved.

But she gave me the one she never had. She gave me what she never got.

CHAPTER SEVEN

What the Scar Took

The tumor was a surprise. The diagnosis was overdue. The surgery changed everything. It was the moment my body stopped being mine. The day I lost what was left of my smile. The year I almost stopped trying.

They found the tumor by pure luck. I did not go to the neurologist because I felt sick. I went because I did not feel wanted. I had spent the last year trying to figure out what made me so hard to love. I thought maybe it was my weight. My face. My voice. I thought if I could just get an answer, I could fix it.

But that doubt is what saved me.

Because it got me into that exam room. And eventually, under that MRI machine.

I had tremors in my hands. My eyes crossed and would not track together.

The left side of my mouth was paralyzed.

I had lived with those symptoms since birth, but back in the late eighties, they just called it neurological deficits. I needed more than that now. I needed a real name. A real diagnosis. Something to hold on to.

What they found instead was a tumor. And to get to it, the surgeon would have to go through the facial nerve.

I was also finally diagnosed with Moebius syndrome, not at birth, but now, after years of being labeled with nothing more than neurological deficits.

But that did not come until later. First came the surgery.

The night before, I made goodbye videos for my kids. Just in case. I tried to be strong. I tried to smile, even though it never came easy for me, not even before. I told them I loved them. I told them how proud I was to be their mama. And I said the things you say when you are not sure you will ever see their faces again.

I deleted those videos. But I can still feel the way it hurt to make them.

The morning of surgery, I pushed John away. Not because I did not want him close, but because I did not know how to ask him to hold on tighter. He let me go too easily. And I went under anesthesia carrying that loneliness with me.

When I opened my eyes, the pain was indescribable. And I was furious.

The surgeon had done what needed to be done. He removed the tumor and cut through what he had to. But in the process, the facial nerve took the hit. My left eye would not close. My mouth barely moved. The face I saw in the mirror did not look like mine. And worse, it did not feel like me.

They said it was the drugs talking when I whispered that I wished I had died. But deep down, I knew it was not just the medication. It was the shock. The grief. The agony. I was warned not to say things like that, told I would end up in the psych ward if I kept it up. So I blamed the anesthesia. Bit my tongue. Swallowed it down.

And from that moment on, I learned how to hide it. I tried to function. Tried to parent. Tried to show up. But I was drowning.

My body was in constant pain. Sharp. Aching. Burning. My face was numb but somehow still hurt. Eating was a challenge. Drinking even harder. I drooled without meaning to. I choked on water. Even that betrayed me. I avoided mirrors. And I gained weight, a lot of it. Because sometimes food was the only thing I could still feel.

People told me I was lucky to be alive. And I was.

But there were days I did not know why God had not just let me go.

I tried to trust Him. I really did. I prayed. I held on. But I was scared. I was scared He was going to take me from my babies. And I could not understand why a God who loved me would let me hurt that much. The pain was relentless. The loneliness was worse. And the one person who had always taken care of me when I was sick, my mama, was gone.

No one rubbed my head or sat by my bed. No one brought me crackers or wiped my tears or whispered that I was going to be okay. I needed her in a way I had not since I was a child. But she was not there.

One night in the middle of all of it, I dreamed of her.

She was not watching me suffer. That is not how heaven works. There is no pain there. No sorrow. I do not believe she saw what I was going through.

But in the dream, she stood in a field of tall sunflowers, smiling the way she used to when something was about to make her laugh. She did not speak. She just opened her arms. And somehow, I felt peace.

I think God let her come close, not to witness my pain, but to remind me that I was still hers. That I was still held.

And maybe more than that. Maybe God used her in that dream to remind me that my work here was not done. Because I was starting to give up. I was tired. I was worn thin. But that dream was a whisper to my soul. A way of saying, not yet. Stay. Your babies still need you. There is more to do.

The scars were not small. One runs from the edge of my nose to the left corner of my mouth, where they later tried to lift what was left. Another stretches from the top of my left ear, down my neck, and under my chin. Every time I looked in the mirror, I saw them. And not just the physical ones.

People told me I was strong. But I felt like I had died and just kept waking up anyway.

This is not where the healing happened.

This is where I shattered.

Where I carried two four-year-olds on my hip and a husband who did not know how to reach me and a son who still needed his mama to show up, and I did. But barely.

James was just a boy back then. He could not carry me, not with his arms. But he carried me anyway. With his laughter. His gentleness. His quiet understanding.

Years later, after another hospital stay left me weak and frail, he was eighteen and strong. He carried me in from the car and laid me gently on the couch when I could not walk.

But he was just as strong in 2016. Because even though he could not lift me then, he still held me together.

And then, one day, Elise looked at me with all the wisdom her preschool-sized body could hold and said, "Girls may not can stand up like boys when they pee. And that is too bad, because standing up to pee is super cool. But girls never give up. Mom, boys may give up, but girls never give up. And that means we win."

It took everything in me not to fall apart right then. Because somehow, even when I could not be brave, my girl was.

I survived because I had to. But maybe I also survived because she believed I would.

The surgery took the tumor. But it took so much more. It took my strength. My certainty. My smile. What little I had left of it.

But I survived. And maybe that is where the story begins again.

CHAPTER EIGHT

You're Not a Burden, But You Are Heavy

For Lee Ann Shaum, who has walked through fire and still shows up with grace. You carry more than most will ever know, and you do it with a kind of quiet courage that humbles me. I am grateful to walk beside you.

There is a certain kind of quiet ache that comes from being the one who always needs taking care of. I feel it when we are out somewhere and John instinctively reaches to steady me. When Erin grabs my plate or checks to see if I need to sit down. When everyone else is walking ahead and I am just trying to keep up, pretending not to notice how much slower I am.

I do not resent their help. I am grateful. Truly. But there is still a part of me that grieves it.

Because I want to be the strong one. The helper. The one other people lean on. Not the one who is tired before the night begins.

Not the one who has to weigh every decision against her body's limits.

Not the one who feels like the grandma of the group, even when she is not.

Just this morning, my friend Lee Ann said those exact words to me.

She told me how hard it is to go out with her best friend and their husbands. How she feels like the grandma in the group.

Not because of her age, but because of everything her body has been through. The near-death experiences. The surgeries. The pain that never fully leaves.

And when she said it, I felt something inside me loosen. Because she named it. The thing I had not had words for. The longing to belong without being a burden.

The heartbreak of being deeply loved and still feeling like too much.

We both know what it is like to feel grateful and invisible all at once. To smile and participate and laugh at the right times, while part of us wonders if we are just the tagalong. The one people accommodate instead of truly invite.

And then there is the guilt. The guilt for needing help.

The guilt for being the one who changes the plan.

The guilt for not being able to do what everyone else can.

The guilt for grieving a body that is still alive, just different now.

Sometimes I try to talk myself out of it.

I tell myself it is not that bad. That I am lucky. That other people have it worse. But pain does not work on a comparison scale. And grief does not listen to logic.

What I have learned, what I am still learning, is that people can love you and still not understand how heavy it feels to need them.

John would never call me a burden. Erin would fight anyone who said I was. But that does not mean I do not feel like one sometimes.

Because it is not about what they say. It is about what I carry.

And the truth is, I am heavy. Not just my body. My needs. My past. My fears. The things I do not always say out loud.

But being heavy does not mean I am unworthy of love.

It just means I need people who are strong enough to carry me sometimes and kind enough not to make me feel small for it.

My mama never let me believe I was fragile.

She knew the world was going to make me feel like I did not belong, like I was not enough, like I would always be a step behind. And she met that reality with fire.

She did not coddle me. She pushed me.

She told me I could do anything anyone else could do, even if I had to do it differently. And when the world tried to write me off, she grabbed the pen back.

She refused to let me settle.

She made sure I knew I had worth, even when no one else saw it.

And she never let me use my disability as an excuse. Not because she lacked compassion, but because she had a fierce kind of belief in me that I sometimes struggled to find in myself.

She wanted me to grow up strong. Independent. Capable. And I did. But now, some days, I feel like I am failing her.

Because I am not strong every day.

Because sometimes I do need help, and I hate how much that bothers me.

Because I know if she were here, she would fight anyone who made me feel like a burden. But I also know she would still be the one carrying half my weight.

And now that weight falls on other people.

On Erin, who does not always know what I need but still tries. And on John, who somehow always does.

He is my constant. The one who anticipates the moment before I say it out loud. The one who can hear what I am not saying. He knows when I am pushing through pain. He knows when I am about to shut down. And he shows up, steady and quiet, like it is second nature. Like loving me never asked too much of him.

But that is what makes it harder. Because I wonder if he is tired too.

If it wears on him, having to be the strong one all the time.

If he ever misses the version of me that was not so dependent.

I try not to say those thoughts out loud.

Not because I want to hide from him, but because I want to protect him from the weight I carry about the weight I carry.

There is a guilt that lives under my skin. So familiar I barely notice it most days.

But it is there. In every moment I sit out. In every event I have to leave early. In every reminder that my body cannot keep up.

And with that guilt comes something even darker. The whisper that maybe I am not enough.

That maybe the people who love me deserve someone easier to love.

That maybe I have become too much. Too complicated. Too heavy.

It is hard to admit that out loud, because I know it is not true.

But some days, truth does not feel louder than shame.

Especially when the world keeps rewarding self-sufficiency and strength and energy I just do not have.

Especially when even the people who love me forget, sometimes, that showing up at all takes everything I have got.

And what does that do to your self-worth? It eats at it.

Slowly. Quietly. Like rust.

Not all at once. But over time, you start to believe that needing help makes you lesser. That if you cannot carry the same weight everyone else does, maybe you do not get the same say.

You become afraid to take up space. To ask for help.

To be seen.

Because somewhere deep down, you start confusing love with tolerance. You stop asking, do they love me?

And start wondering, how much more of me can they handle?

And sometimes, even love that is meant to protect you starts to sound like proof that you are not enough.

John is steady. He is gentle. He sees me when others do not.

But every now and then, out of concern, he tells me I should not do something. Or says he will just do it for me.

He means well. I know that.

He is trying to spare me pain, prevent a fall, ease the strain.

But the part of me that already feels like a burden hears something else. It hears, you cannot.

It hears, you are not capable.

It hears, you are the one we have to plan around. The one who always needs help.

He is not trying to hurt me.

But it still stings.

Because even when the words come wrapped in love, they leave behind something sharp.

And I hate that.

I hate that I get hurt by someone trying to help.

I hate that I am so tender in that place, that wounded part of me that still thinks my worth is tied to what I can do.

When he lifts something heavy, I do not feel grateful. I feel weak.

When he says, "Don't worry about it, I've got it," I do not feel supported. I feel invisible.

When he tells me not to push myself, I wonder if he thinks I am already broken.

It is not his fault.

It is the fault of a world that told me needing someone made me less. It is the fault of all the times I have had to prove I belonged.

It is the fault of a lifetime of internalizing that strength means silence, independence, and pushing through pain without complaint.

Sometimes the hardest part of needing help is not the asking. It is the wondering. How will they look at me when I do?

Will they sigh?

Will they act like it is a chore?

Will they make me feel small for needing something I cannot do alone?

There are nights I lie there staring at the ceiling, knowing I cannot even unhook my own bra. And I debate whether to ask for help or just sleep in it and wake up sore. Not because I want to prove anything. But because the ache of needing someone who is upset with me sometimes hurts worse than the straps digging into my back.

And that is the part no one talks about.

When your body does not cooperate and your heart already feels tender, even the smallest ask can feel like a risk. A gamble. A moment where love might not show up the way you need it to.

I still want to be strong. But more than that, I want to be safe to need what I need. Because being a burden is not about asking.

It is about being made to feel like the asking is too much.

And I do complain sometimes.

I cry. I sit down. I say no.

And when I do, there is a voice in the back of my head asking if I have disappointed someone again.

Even the people who love me most. Especially them.

But the hardest part?

It is not John.

It is not Erin.

It is my kids.

I am supposed to be the one taking care of them.

I am their mother. Their soft place to land. Their steady ground.

And I do everything I can to show up that way. But sometimes my body betrays me.

And they end up holding me up instead.

Like at the beach.

I was never great in the sand, even when I was younger. But now? Now it is nearly impossible.

The uneven ground. The heat. The way the grains shift under my feet with every step. It is not just inconvenient. It is dangerous.

And I watch them watching me, trying to help, trying to adjust, when they should just be running ahead and laughing, carefree.

My children pay the price for a body that does not work like it should.

They pay every time they have to put the cart away for me in the rain because I might slip.

They pay every time they have to slow down because I cannot keep up.

They pay when they reach for my hand, not because they are scared, but because I am.

They do not complain.

They just love me.

But I see it.

I feel it.

And it wrecks me.

Because I wanted to be the fun mom. The strong mom.

The mom who could chase them down the beach and carry all the towels and walk back to the car without needing a break.

Instead, I am the mom who sits down too soon. The mom who is always tired.

The mom who gets left behind, not because they want to, but because I tell them to go ahead.

And they do. Because they are kind. Because they are good.

But every step they take without me chips away at the version of motherhood I thought I would give them.

And the hardest part is knowing they do not see it that way.

They do not see me as a burden. They do not act resentful or distant. They just keep adjusting. Quietly. Lovingly. Automatically.

And I hate that they have had to.

I hate that their childhood has been shaped by the things I cannot do.

That they have learned to scan a room for obstacles, to check the ground before I step, to read my face for signs of pain.

They should not have to do that. They should just get to be kids.

I worry sometimes about what they will remember.

Not just about the days we sat things out or left early or skipped altogether, but about how it felt to always consider someone else's body when they were still figuring out their own.

I wonder if it will make them stronger. Or if it will make them tired.

I hope it builds compassion.

I just hope it does not build resentment.

Because I never wanted them to feel like I was their responsibility. I just wanted to be their mom.

The soft place to land. The strong arms. The one who carried, not the one who had to be carried.

And I know I still give them love. I know I still show up.

But some nights, I lie awake wishing I could go back and give them more of the version of me that did not have to pause before every yes.

And all I can do now is hope they will see what I tried to give them even when my body gave out.

That they will remember the way I looked at them like they were my whole world. That they will feel the way I cheered for them, even from the sidelines.

That they will carry the love, not the weight.

I think part of why all of this wrecks me so deeply is because I have been on the other side of it.

I was the child who needed more.

I was the one who did not hit milestones.

The one who could not walk on time or talk on time.

The one who came with hospital visits and surgeries and feeding struggles and a future no doctor could predict.

I was the child people whispered about. The one strangers stared at. The one teachers doubted. The one other moms pitied.

And my mama carried it all.

She carried me, literally and emotionally and spiritually.

She fought the school system. She argued with doctors. She refused to let anyone reduce me to a diagnosis.

She made sure I did not grow up feeling less than.

But now that I am a mom myself, I wonder about the things she never said.

Did she cry in the car after dropping me off at school, knowing how hard it was going to be for me?

Did she sit alone in the living room at night and wonder what my future would look like, if I would have friends, if I would fall in love, if the world would ever see me the way she did?

Did she ever wish it had been easier?

She never made me feel like a burden. Never.

But I wonder if I was one anyway.

I wonder if there were days she just wanted to breathe without thinking about therapies or money or appointments or how to make me feel beautiful when the world did not treat me that way.

I wonder if she ever looked at other moms who got to pack dance bags and soccer cleats and felt that ache of everything she did not get.

I do not know.

Because she did not let me see that part. She smiled. She pushed. She protected.

She made cookies when I could not go ride bikes like the other kids. She found joy in places that did not require walking.

She loved me so loudly that I never had to question it.

But now that I am the one sitting in the shade, the one watching from the sidelines, the one adjusting plans so my kids do not have to see how much it hurts, I get it.

And it haunts me sometimes.

I hope I did not take too much from her.

I hope I was not the reason she missed out on the life she dreamed of.

I hope I gave her laughter and light and pride and purpose.

I hope I made her feel needed and treasured and strong.

Because now that I know what this kind of love costs, I do not just feel grateful.

I feel gutted.

Because I know what she gave up. And I know what she poured out.

And I never want her to think it was not worth it.

If I did not say it then, I am saying it now.

Mama, I saw it.

Even when I was too little to understand. Even when I did not have the words.

I saw the way you loved me. I felt it in the way you stayed.

In the way you held it all together.

In the way you chose me, over and over, when the world told you I would never be enough.

You gave me everything.

And I hope, in some small way, I gave you something beautiful too.

Thank you, Mama.

For fighting when I could not.

For believing when no one else did.

For making a life that felt full, even when it was hard. For giving me a childhood wrapped in love and defiance and fierce protection.

I know it was not easy. I know I asked more of you than you ever planned for. And still, you gave. You did not just carry me.

You taught me how to carry others. And I am who I am because you stayed. You were my first home. My safest place. And every time I reach for strength now, I find yours in me.

Remember When

A love letter to the man who stayed, even when everything changed.

John,

Sometimes I do not know how to say thank you. Not in a way that feels big enough. Not in a way that touches all the places you have quietly carried me through.

We have lived a thousand lives together. I still remember the first one. The early years when we had more bills than dollars and a twin bed that somehow fit your six-foot-three frame and my soft, oversized body. You would sleep with your leg draped over mine like a spoon. From your knee to your foot was as long as my whole leg, even bent. It sounds impossible now, but it felt like comfort then. It felt like home.

Our kids do not believe half the things we lived through. But we know.

You have walked beside me through so much. Through rejection that left me raw. Through the kind of grief that changed me forever. When my mama died, it was your steady presence that helped me find my footing. When James was born and everything shifted. When the twins came and our world exploded into exhaustion and chaos and love. You held me through it all.

And I have watched you be a father in the ways that matter most. You are the one who brings the laughter. The one who turns ordinary moments into memories. You expect a lot from them, but you always show up. You are steady, and they know you are theirs.

And even when we broke, when we hurt each other in ways we do not talk about often, you still stayed. You helped bring me through that too. Maybe we brought each other through.

Staying is not always soft. Sometimes it is grit. Sometimes it is forgiveness. Sometimes it is choosing the same person again, even after everything changes. We have done that. Over and over.

You never stopped showing up. Even when I was unraveling. Even when I lost what was left of the half smile I had. When half my face gave up completely and nothing felt like mine anymore, you did not look at me like something had been taken. You looked at me like I was still the girl you married. You made me feel beautiful when I could barely look at myself.

You have seen every version of me. The sick. The scared. The struggling. The woman who used to cry over numbers on a scale and now cries because her blood sugar will not behave or her eyes will not adjust. You have carried me, truly carried me, when I could not walk. You have read the words I could not see. You have helped me navigate a world that gets blurrier every day. In so many ways, you have become my eyes. You have helped me keep moving forward when I was not sure I could.

And now, as life shifts again and the unknown sits quietly between us, I hope you know I will be beside you through all of it. Whatever comes, I am here. Just like you have always been for me.

You say it best when you say nothing at all. And after more than twenty-five years, that song is still ours. It still tells the truth. We do not always need the words. I hear you in the way you hold my hand. I see you in the way you show up. I feel you in every quiet act of love.

This letter does not come close to the love notes you have written me over the years. Mine are flat compared to yours. But I needed you to know. Even if I cannot say it the way you would have. Even if I stumble over every word.

We remember when it was all so new. When we swore we would never change. And even though everything has changed, some things have not. You still reach for me in the dark. And I still feel safest when you do.

Maybe growing older will not feel so scary after all. Not if we are still remembering when, and still choosing now. We will not be sad. We will be glad for all the life we have had. And we will remember when.

You gave me my greatest story. Not because it was easy. But because it was real. And because you stayed.

Love, Tina

CHAPTER NINE

I Didn't Feel Chosen

There was a season in my life when I didn't feel like anyone's first choice. Not even in my own home. Not even in my own skin. I had three kids. One in elementary school, two still in diapers. The days were loud. The house was always messy. And I felt like I was holding everything together with a rubber band and a prayer.

I was exhausted. Not just physically. Deeply. Emotionally. Quietly.

I don't remember the exact moment things shifted. I just remember feeling like something between us had changed. I couldn't explain it.

There were no big arguments or breaking points. Just a growing distance I didn't know how to close. We still had good days. We still laughed sometimes.

But I started to feel more like a roommate than a wife. More like a manager than a partner.

More like a body than a person.

There were moments I looked at him and wondered if he would still choose me, if he ever had.

I wanted more, but I didn't know how to ask for it without sounding ungrateful. He was working hard. I was home with the kids.

We were doing everything we were supposed to do. But I still felt invisible. And when you go too long without feeling chosen, you start to question everything. Not just your marriage.

Your worth. Your strength. Your value as a woman. I never stopped loving my family. But I started losing pieces of myself I didn't know how to get back.

I wasn't unhappy every day. It wasn't dramatic like that. Most days looked normal from the outside. I made lunch. Wiped faces. Picked up toys I had already picked up three times before. I answered questions. I rocked babies. I managed the chaos.

I did what moms do. My joints ached. My back throbbed. There were days I limped through the house holding a baby on each hip and a scream in my throat, praying just to make it to bedtime. But inside, I was unraveling.

I used to be someone. Not in a flashy way. But in a way that felt alive. Like I mattered. Like someone wanted to know me, not just need me. But in that season, it felt like all I did was meet needs. I filled cups and plates and prescriptions, and somewhere along the way, I stopped remembering what it felt like to be full myself.

I didn't feel beautiful. I didn't feel smart. I didn't feel like I brought anything special into a room. I felt heavy. Foggy. Tired.

I missed the girl I used to be. The one who laughed without guilt. Who felt wanted instead of useful. Who knew her own name without it being followed by Mom. And the worst part was that I started to believe maybe this was just the tradeoff. Maybe you give up being seen when you become the one everyone depends on.

I didn't want to feel that way. I wanted to feel proud of all I was doing. I wanted to feel like a good wife. A good mom. A good woman. But instead, I felt like I was quietly failing at everything.

The house was never clean enough. The laundry was never caught up. I couldn't fix the tired look on my face, no matter how much I tried to cover it. And I could feel the tension growing between us.

He never said he resented me. But I felt it. In the sighs. In the silence. In the way I could tell he was waiting for me to do better, be better, carry more. And I was trying. God, I was trying.

But no matter what I did, it never felt like enough. And I started to believe that maybe I wasn't enough either. We were both hurting. Both carrying things we didn't know how to say out loud. And in that silence, we hurt each other in the most devastating ways. Not with shouting. Not with slammed doors. But with distance. With absence. With quiet choices that left bruises no one could see.

Not because we did not love each other. But because we did not know how to love each other through the loneliness we were living in.

We were two people trying to hold a life together while slowly falling apart inside it. And when you are that broken, even the smallest things start to feel like confirmation that you are the problem.

A look. A missed call. A too-long silence.

It all felt personal. Even when it wasn't. And what hurt the most wasn't the anger. It was the ache of knowing we didn't feel safe with each other anymore.

I didn't trust that he still saw me. And maybe he didn't trust me with his pain either. Maybe we were both guarding wounds we never learned how to tend together.

And still, life didn't pause. There were lunches to pack. Diapers to change. Baths to run. Fights to settle. Bedtime stories to read even when all I wanted to do was crawl into bed and disappear.

I had to keep moving. There wasn't space to fall apart. Not when someone always needed something from me. Not when I was the one holding it all up.

So I pushed it down. The loneliness. The guilt. The shame.

I buried it under loads of laundry and carpool lines. I swallowed it while heating up chicken nuggets and filling sippy cups. And I smiled for my kids, because they didn't need to know that their mother was unraveling. They were the reason I kept standing. Even when I was sure I couldn't.

I still don't know how I made it through some of those days. The exhaustion was more than physical. It was spiritual. Emotional. Like I was stretched so thin there wasn't even room to feel anymore. Just perform.

Just survive. Just get to bedtime without breaking in front of them. I would stand in the shower with the water too hot, just to feel something that didn't ask anything of me. But even when the house was loud, I felt alone. Even when I was surrounded, I felt unseen.

That's what no one talks about. That you can love your children with your whole soul and still feel like you are disappearing inside your own life.

That you can be grateful and broken at the same time.

I knew we weren't okay. I knew I wasn't okay. But there was never a good time to say it. Never a clean way to confess the pain without setting something on fire.

So I kept going. And I kept shrinking. And I told myself this was just what marriage looked like after kids. After years. After so much unspoken hurt. But deep down, I missed being known. Not needed.

Not relied on. Just known. And I didn't know how to get that back. We tried not to fight in front of the kids. But sometimes we did.

The tension got too heavy. The silence too loud. Even when we were trying to protect them, it spilled out in small ways. And they knew. Kids always know. James was still young, but he noticed. He watched everything. He may not have had the words, but I could see it in his eyes. He felt the distance. He felt the shift. He would sometimes come sit beside me without saying a word. Just sit there. Like he knew I needed someone to remind me I was still there too.

There was one week I'll never forget. He told the kids Daddy was going on a business trip. But really, he was staying at a hotel just down the road. A few miles. Not hours. I brought him his clothes in a plastic bag. There was no big scene. No yelling. Just me in a parking lot, handing him what he needed. And when he came home, like he always did, he said thank you. He said, "Thank you for always letting me come home." And I nodded, even though I hadn't always. Because there was a time I locked the door. Not out of rage.

But out of ache. His absence came first. Sudden, sharp, and hard to breathe through. But mine lingered. Mine became a pattern. A rhythm. A place I disappeared into for far too long.

It wasn't equal. It wasn't clean. It wasn't some even exchange of pain. It was just two people who had stopped reaching for each other.

And when you live in that kind of distance long enough, you start building other ways to feel alive. Some are healthy. Some are not. Some stay longer than you ever intended.

We never talked about it. Not directly. Not in the way that would have meant healing at the time. But somehow, even with all of it sitting between us, he still came home. And eventually, I unlocked the door.

Because I still loved him. And somewhere deep down, I think he still loved me too. Even when neither of us looked like the versions we fell in love with. Even when we barely recognized ourselves.

We stayed. That's the part people don't always understand. We stayed in the same house. We ate dinner at the same table. We took care of the same kids. We passed the salt without speaking. We showed up to parent-teacher conferences. We sat side by side at school plays and birthday dinners, pretending everything was fine. We moved forward, because there wasn't really another choice that made sense at the time.

But moving forward doesn't mean things were repaired. It just means we kept going. Some days, we laughed. Other days, we barely spoke. Some nights, we shared the same bed and the same silence. Other nights, I cried in the bathroom with the door locked and the water running.

And through all of it, we were still physically intimate. We didn't stop touching. We didn't stop reaching for each other in the dark, even when we had stopped doing it in the light.

Every once in a while, our hands would brush while passing each other in the kitchen, and for a split second, it felt like neither of us had fully given up. It was complicated. Sometimes it felt like connection. Sometimes it felt like habit. Sometimes it felt like trying to prove something neither of us could say out loud.

We were still showing up in each other's bodies, even when our hearts didn't know how to meet in the middle.

That made it harder, in some ways. Because how do you feel so far apart from someone who still sleeps beside you? How do you feel unseen by someone who still reaches for your hand?

If my mama had still been alive, I think I might have left. Maybe not forever. Maybe I would have packed up the kids and gone to her house for a week or two. Just long enough to remember who I was.

Long enough to feel safe again. Because she would have made room for me. She always did.

I would have had a place to cry. A place to breathe. A place to fall apart without feeling like I was breaking everything else in the process. But she was gone. And instead of refuge, I had silence.

Instead of comfort, I had the weight of three small people who needed me to stay strong. And I did. But it came at a cost.

There were nights when the ache of it all got too loud, and I didn't always handle it well. I still wanted to feel seen. Wanted to feel like I mattered to someone. Like I was more than tired hands and a fading smile.

Days I wanted to run. Days I wondered if we had ruined each other too deeply to come back from. Days I looked at him and thought, you hurt me. And days I looked in the mirror and thought, you hurt him too.

Sometimes, the people you love the most are the ones who can hurt you the deepest. Not because they mean to. But because they matter that much. But we stayed. And over time, the staying became something stronger than the breaking.

It didn't undo the past. It didn't erase the silence, or the mistakes, or the ache that still shows up some nights.

But it gave us something else.

A love that is weathered. A love that knows what it costs to fall and still choose to rise. A love that has been stretched to the edge and still reaches back.

We didn't get a perfect ending. But we got something real. And in a world that gives up too fast, sometimes that is the most sacred kind of love there is.

We're twenty-five years in now. Not because we got everything right. But because, somehow, even after all the silence and hurt and years of wondering if we could come back from it, we did.

We stayed. We rebuilt. We still choose each other.

Maybe not in the same way we did at the beginning, but maybe that's the point.

Because this version of love is deeper. It's quieter. And it knows what it cost to survive.

I didn't just stay. I fought. For myself. For us. For the kind of love that doesn't run from the hard parts.

John is my family. And my mama taught me you don't leave your family. You stay. And you fight.

Because they were watching. And I wanted them to know that even broken things can be worth saving. And I keep choosing it. Not because it is easy. But because it is ours.

CHAPTER TEN

This Time I Chose Me

The world didn't get smaller. I did. Not in the way people think, though. Not because I hated myself. I had spent my whole life doing that. This time, I was fighting for her. The version of me buried under shame and stretch marks. The one who had always been waiting to be chosen.

It started during the long, slow ache of the pandemic. We were all home. All stuck. All quietly unraveling in our own ways. But I wasn't just bored or restless.

I was starving for something. Maybe to feel seen. Maybe to feel wanted. Maybe to feel like I could still be chosen.

Yes, I had a husband. But that doesn't mean I always felt chosen. Not in the way I was aching for. Not in the way that made me feel alive. So I started choosing myself.

At first, I didn't even realize I was eating less. There wasn't some big plan. No strict routine. I just knew I couldn't keep feeling the way I felt. I needed something to change. And for the first time, it wasn't about disappearing. It was about waking up.

About taking control of something. About reaching for a version of me I hadn't seen in a long time. Maybe ever.

When I first started my weight loss journey, I'd stay up late watching My 600-lb Life. Instead of eating tacos or pasta, I'd microwave a Just Crack an Egg cup and tell myself that was enough. And I'd sit there stunned that every single person on that show had a significant other. Someone who was still with them.

Some of those partners were deeply loving. Some were bitter. Some were checked out. But almost all of them had to do everything for their person. Wipe them. Bathe them. Carry the weight. And I'd think about how John has always taken care of me.

Especially when I've been sick. Especially when I've been knocking on death's door. But even then, I knew this:

I'd never let him wipe my ass because I got too big to reach it myself. Not because he wouldn't do it. I know he would.

But because I loved him too much to put him in that position.

And maybe I was being dramatic. I wasn't even close to being that big or to that point, but I loved myself enough not to go any further in the wrong direction.

I'd been trying to lose weight for as far back as I could remember.

When I was six years old, I overheard my Aunt Margaret tell my mom I was too chubby to wear a two-piece swimsuit.

When I was five, maybe younger, my Mamaw started offering to buy me a whole new wardrobe if I could just lose the weight.

She meant well. But I learned early that being smaller was something you had to earn, and I never quite managed to deserve it.

I've been fighting my body my whole life. As a little girl, I had to shop in the Pretty Plus section at Sears. That was the polite way of saying big, but it still made me feel like I didn't fit.

My mama didn't mean to, but I think she taught me early on that food could be a kind of comfort.

When I couldn't go outside and ride a bike like the other kids, she'd make cookies with me instead. When I was hurting, she gave me something warm to eat. When I was lonely or left out, we'd bake or snack or find something to enjoy together. Food became our way of saying we were okay. It became entertainment, comfort, connection. And eventually, it became the way I coped when she was gone. I don't blame her. She was doing the best she could.

But I learned early that food could soothe, and I carried that with me. Mamaw said the same things again when I was ten. Thirteen. Sixteen. I never could lose the weight.

And I carried that failure like a scar. And I had been made to fight to live, over and over again. Through surgeries. Through sickness. Through sadness that sat too long in my bones. Even after I lost the weight, I was still fighting. But The weight was something I could control. That was something I could do something about.

And eventually, I just didn't want to fight that anymore.

I've never trusted my body to obey me.

But for once, I made it listen. For once, it wasn't my illness or my scars calling the shots. It was me.

It wasn't just about looks. It was about staying here. I didn't want to go out early like my mama did. I didn't want my kids standing at my grave wishing they had more time. If I leave this world too soon, I sure as hell don't want it to be because of something I could've prevented.

Something I had control over. I don't want to go down without a fight. I knew being fat was killing me. Slowly. Quietly. And I wanted to live. I wanted to stay.

This wasn't about chasing skinny. It was about outrunning the grave. About fighting back against a body that had tried to take me too many times already. But every other time I'd tried to lose weight, and there were so many, I wasn't trying to live. I was trying to be wanted. To be looked at. To be chosen.

I tried everything.

The cabbage soup diet—the one where you eat nothing but fruit one day, a plain baked potato the next, and try not to pass out in between.

When I was sixteen, I punished myself with a starvation I called discipline: one cup of plain white rice with soy sauce a day. Two servings of sugar-free Jell-O. That was it.

No protein. No fat. No carbs. No joy. Just hunger and shame and the scale. In college, it got worse. I'd eat one cereal bar and tell myself that was enough. I'd go to bed dizzy, wake up shaking, and convince myself I was strong. Until I couldn't take it anymore and I'd end up in the Jack in the Box drive-thru, ordering bacon cheddar potato wedges with extra cheese.

I'd eat until I was nauseous. Then cry. Then start starving all over again.

I tried diet pills. The kind that made my heart race and my hands tremble. I told myself that meant they were working. I even got the lap band. And yes, I lost weight. But not because I wasn't hungry. Because I was terrified to eat.

Food got stuck. Water got stuck. It would sit in my chest like a brick, unmoving, unspit, unswallowed. I couldn't push it down. I couldn't bring it back up. Eventually, the only thing I could safely drink was scalding hot liquid. Even soup had to burn.

John has written me love notes over the years. So many. He used to be so romantic. But the kindest thing he ever said to me might have been on an ordinary day, while we were watching The Biggest Loser.

I said I wished I could lose ten or fifteen pounds in a week like they did. He looked at me and said, "*Tina, you are not them. You are not nearly as big as they are.*" I was probably still around 240 pounds.

But in that moment, I felt seen. I felt cared for. Even now, I sometimes wonder if John preferred me heavier. Not because he ever said that. But because when I first started losing weight, he'd say things like, "*You sure you don't want a bite of this?*"

I used to tease him and call him a chubby chaser. He swears he only asked because he was worried I was doing without, he loves me, and wants to share the good things he has. Now he goes out of his way to make sure I eat and stay hydrated.

I'm really bad about drinking enough water, and some days I wake up dizzy and weak. But he always notices. He always takes care of me.

He sends me to concerts with my friends. Tells me to get my nails done. He wants me to have a good life.

He knows how hard I am on myself, and even when he doesn't say much, I know he's trying to make space for me to feel joy. I'm trying to receive it.

I always go from one extreme to another. I'll starve, or I'll binge. But For the first time in my life, I'm finding balance. And for the first time in my life, I'm choosing me so I can be here for the people I love.

I've worked so hard to make peace with my body. But I still get overwhelmed in places like buffets. I feel like everyone is watching me.

Like they're thinking, *look at that fat woman with all that food on her plate.* Or look *how many times she's gone back.*

Even when I was just getting food for my kids, I'd feel the shame settle in my chest. They were too little to carry their own plates, so I'd go back again and again. But I just knew people thought I was eating it all.

Even now, though I'm much smaller, the shame still follows me to those places. It's a voice I can't always silence.

And it hurts more than I like to admit.

Every time I go to a concert, I still try to buy an XL or 2X shirt. I hold it up like a safety blanket. But Erin always steps in and tells me I don't need that size anymore. She'll hold up a large or sometimes even a medium and say, "Tina, this is what you wear now." And she's usually right.

But my brain still sees the bigger version of me. Still expects the fit I used to need.

There was a time I couldn't fit comfortably in a restaurant booth at Chili's. I was pregnant with twins. And I know that should explain it, but it didn't make it less humiliating. I had to ask to be moved to a table with chairs.

Erin was with me and tried to comfort me. She reminded me I was carrying two babies. But all I could feel was shame. All I could think about was how big I must have looked. It was one of the most embarrassing moments of my life. And then there was the time I went to Six Flags.

I used to be terrified the seatbelt on the ride wouldn't buckle. Even after I lost the weight, that fear didn't go away.

But one day, it buckled easily. I had room to tighten it.

And I felt something I hadn't felt in years. Free.

I didn't laugh, because I can't. But I smiled with my eyes.

And in that moment, I felt proud. Not because I looked good.

But because I didn't have to ask for a different seat. Because for once, I fit.

Some days I don't even know why I try. I could have the body. The muscles. The stomach tucked flat. But I will never be pretty. Not in the way this world defines it. Because my face is paralyzed.

Because I was born with something that made people stare before I ever learned to walk. There's no glow-up. No transformation. And maybe that's why I didn't value my body for so long. Because no matter how much progress I made, I'd still have this face. The one people look away from.

The one they talk over. The one that made me believe I didn't matter. I'm trying to be okay with it. But most days, I'm not.

Some people worry about gaining ten pounds. I worry about the fact that I can't smile. Not just that I don't like my smile. I physically can't. I wonder if people think I'm cold or rude because my face won't move the way they expect it to.

Because I can't give them what they're looking for.

But I am kind. I am funny. I am soft where it counts. People just don't always see that. They just see my face.

I once heard someone whisper, "She should do something about her stomach."

As if the stretch marks and loose skin were something to erase instead of proof that I fought like hell to stay.

I'll never be what the world calls beautiful. But this body? This body kept me alive. And I am learning to love what I choose.

Not what others see. But what I've taken back for myself. Every tattoo. Every scar. Every ounce of softness that has stayed. They are mine.

Not because I love them yet. But because I survived in them.

Most days, I still feel like I'll never be thin enough. Never be enough *enough.*

But that's when I try to stand on the only thing that doesn't change. God's Word.

Romans 5:8 says that God proved His love for me in this: while I was still a sinner, Christ died for me.

Not once I got it together. Not once I was thin. But while I was still broken. Still bingeing. Still ashamed.

Psalm 139:14 says I am fearfully and wonderfully made. Even when I don't feel like it.

Even when I fail. Even now. This time, I chose me. Not to be seen. But to stay. And I will keep choosing her. Even when it's hard. Even when I forget. Especially then.

This wasn't the end of anything. It was the beginning of me telling the truth. And here's one more truth. Losing the weight didn't fix everything. My medical issues didn't disappear. I didn't wake up healed or whole or brand new. Some pain stayed.

Some problems followed. Some days, my body still fights me. But I am still here. And I am still fighting back. And if you're reading this, if you've ever felt like you're too far gone, too broken, too big, too messy, too tired, I want you to know something. *You are still worthy.* Right now. As you are.

You don't have to disappear to be loved. You don't have to earn your place. I didn't know it then, but Jesus had already set a place for me. Even when I was fat. Even when I couldn't see it. Even when I didn't believe I belonged anywhere. He still said, come.

And He meant me. He means you, too. Choosing yourself doesn't mean you have it all figured out. It just means you finally stopped waiting for someone else to do it for you.

So if no one else tells you today, you are not too much. You are not too late. You don't have to get smaller to take up space in this world. There is room for you here. There always was.

CHAPTER ELEVEN

Finding My Way Home

There was a moment when I thought everything might fall apart. A shift I could not name, but I felt it. Deep in my body, like the air between us had changed.

There was distance. Disappointment. Things we never fully said but both knew.

And for a while, I wondered if we would make it. If love was enough.

If history could hold what hurt had hollowed out.

I did not leave. Not physically. But part of me pulled back, just to survive the weight of it all.

Still, I stayed.

Because I needed him. Because the kids needed him.

Because he was all I had ever known, and the thought of unraveling what we had built felt too heavy to carry alone.

But somewhere in the quiet that followed, I realized something else.

I could have made it on my own if I needed to. I was not staying because I was weak. I was not staying because I could not survive without him.

I stayed because I loved him. Not just because I needed him. And that changed everything.

It was the first time I understood that love is not about dependency. It is about choosing someone even when you know you could stand without them.

And I chose him. Not out of habit. Not out of fear. But because even after everything, I still wanted to build something real with the person I had nearly lost. Not because it was easy. Not because everything felt right again. But because something in me needed to try.

To rebuild. To see if the life we had could still hold the people we were becoming. And because love, real love, is not a feeling.

It is a choice. A hard one. An angry one, sometimes.

One you make through gritted teeth when the feelings have packed up and left, but the vows are still sitting in the room with you.

Love is not butterflies or fireworks or breathless passion. Not here. Not anymore. Sometimes it is folding laundry when you would rather scream. Sometimes it is sitting in silence because talking feels impossible. Sometimes it is staying when the world would understand if you left.

Feelings come and go. But love, if it is going to last, has to be chosen again and again. Even when it is bruised.

Even when it is quiet. Even when it does not look like the love you hoped for. And somewhere in the middle of all that staying, I had to face something else too.

I needed forgiveness too. Not just for what I had done. But for the way I had shut down. For the ways I had disappeared inside myself. For the parts of me I withheld, even when I said I was still trying.

Because hurt people do not just bleed. Sometimes they go numb. Sometimes they protect themselves by building walls so high that even love cannot climb over.

So I stayed. And I started turning inward. I could not wait for something outside of me to feel like home again. So I began making peace inside the parts of me that still ached.

I asked myself what healing might look like if I stopped chasing resolution and started reclaiming rest. And maybe that is where it began. Not with forgetting. Not even with forgiving.

But with the smallest kind of hope. The kind that says I did not have to stay lost just because something between us had been.

It did not look like much at first. Healing rarely does. It looked like getting out of bed when it would have been easier to stay under the covers.

It looked like driving the kids to school when my chest still felt heavy. It looked like cooking dinner when no one had said sorry yet.

It was not about fixing the marriage. It was about not forgetting myself inside of it.

Because somewhere along the way, I had started disappearing. I had become the peacekeeper. The one who smoothed things over. The one who tried to hold everything together before it cracked.

I had become the forgiver. But the truth is, I needed forgiveness too. For the things I had done.

For the pain I had caused in return. For the ways I had shut down, even when I said I was still trying. Because hurt does not always come with yelling. Sometimes it comes with silence. With going through the motions. With letting resentment grow roots because you are too tired to dig them up. And the hardest part was how different we were in the aftermath.

I am the kind of person who cannot sleep when something is broken. I want to stay up all night talking it out, fixing it, making sense of it until the air feels clear again. I want to be held and heard and told it is going to be okay, even if it is not yet.

But he is the kind who needs space. He wants to shut down, cool off, and move on like nothing happened. He will get over it eventually, but without words. Without answers.

And that mismatch, that difference in how we carry pain, almost broke me. Because I did not just want peace.

I wanted connection. I wanted proof that the love was still there beneath the wreckage. So I had to stop waiting for him to come find me in the middle of the storm.

I had to start finding myself again. I did not wait until things were healed to start showing up. Because if I had, I might still be waiting.

So I showed up anyway. I showed up to the school pick-up line with tired eyes and a face no one could read, but I was there. I showed up to their bedrooms at night with a quiet voice and a hand on their back, even when mine felt empty. I showed up in the kitchen, cooking dinner when I did not have the words, but still feeding the people I love.

Some days I did it well. Other days I did it because I did not know what else to do. But I kept showing up.

Not because I felt strong. But because something in me refused to disappear.

They could not always see joy on my face, but it was there in the way I leaned in to listen. They could not always tell when I was proud, but they felt it in the way I spoke their names.

I could not smile like the world expected, but I still loved with my whole being, and that mattered more. I gave grace, even when I was not sure I deserved it. I stayed kind, even when I felt forgotten.

I made room for them to feel safe, even when I did not. And little by little, I started to believe maybe I was still in there. Not the same version of me. But not lost either.

I stopped waiting for someone else to fix what felt broken. And I started asking what it would look like to live from a place of wholeness, even in the middle of the mess.

It did not make everything better overnight. It did not erase the ache. But it reminded me that I was still here. Still loving.

Still trying. Still mine. And slowly, something between us shifted too. Not because he changed overnight.

Not because we had some grand breakthrough or said all the things we had left unsaid. But because I changed.

I stopped begging to be understood and started speaking plainly. I stopped waiting for him to make me feel safe and started becoming a safe place for myself. I stopped twisting myself into someone smaller just to keep the peace. And maybe he noticed.

Or maybe he just missed the version of me that used to carry all the weight in silence.

But over time, the tension softened. Not completely. Not forever. But enough to breathe again.

He started looking at me a little longer when I spoke. He started thanking me for things he used to take for granted. He started sitting beside me in the quiet instead of walking away from it.

We did not talk about what happened. We still have not, not really. But I stopped needing him to say all the right words. Because I was not waiting on his voice to give mine value anymore.

I loved him still. I just stopped needing that love to look a certain way to believe it was real.

We are not what we used to be. But maybe that is not all bad. Maybe there is something honest about love that has been bruised but stayed. Something steady in the choosing. Something sacred in the staying.

We still have days where we miss each other in the same room. Days where the hurt feels louder than the healing. Where he shuts down and I reach too hard. Where I talk too much trying to fix it, and he does not want to say anything at all. But even on those days, we stay.

Sometimes with tenderness. Sometimes with tension. But we stay. Because love is not some soft place we fall into and float around in forever.

Love is work. Love is stubborn. Love is choosing again and again, even when the feelings come and go. And we do love each other. That part never left.

People do not talk about this enough. That the ones who love each other the most are also the ones who can hurt each other the deepest. Not always with intention. But with absence. With distance. With silence when one of you needs closeness the most.

We have hurt each other. We have disappointed each other. But we have also stayed. And grown. And kept finding our way back to one another, even when it was hard.

It might not look like the movies. But it looks like us.

It looks like two people who still reach for each other under the covers at night, even when the day was long.

Two people who carry the weight of the past but still show up anyway.

Two people who are still in love, just not in the shiny, easy, effortless way the world likes to celebrate.

There is history here.

There is hope. And more than anything, there is love.

Because love, for us, is not just something we feel. It is something we do. A choice we both keep making. Even on the days when it is hard.

Especially on the days when it is hard. We are still here. Still building. Still loving. Still choosing.

And above our bed hangs the words he once picked out himself, words that feel even truer now than when we first hung them up:

> *And I would choose you. In a hundred lifetimes. In a hundred worlds. In any version of reality. I would find you. And I would choose you.*

That is what love looks like for us now. Not perfect. But present. Not untouched by pain. But still reaching for each other anyway. And in all the ways that matter, I found my way home.

CHAPTER TWELVE

You'd Have Had a Place at Her Table

They told my mama I would be completely blind by the time I was sixteen. They taught me braille. She braced herself for a life of guiding me through darkness, of never seeing my face light up or watching me read a book or find my way across a room.

But I believed in a God who could do anything. And somehow, my vision stayed. God healed my vision.

There is no other explanation. The doctors had no answers. The charts said one thing, but my life said another. They prepared me for darkness. But God gave me sight.

It was simple back then. I did not need theology or doctrine. I just believed. I believed God healed. I believed He loved me. I believed He saw me.

My mama did too. We did not grow up in church at first, but when I came home one day crying that I was going to hell, she did not brush me off. She called a church. That night. With no appointment.

Pastor Brother Bob welcomed us with open arms and an even more open heart. He did not ask us to wait for Sunday or fill out a form. He just said, come on.

I remember that church office like a second home. I remember felt boards in Sunday School, the smell of old Bibles, the way people smiled at me without staring. For a little while, it was the safest place I knew.

One Sunday morning, my Sunday School teacher said something I never forgot. He told us, if you believe in Jesus and you are wrong, you will still live a good, moral, fulfilled life. But if you are right, you will spend eternity with Him.

Then he looked around the room and said, if you really believe in salvation, if you really believe what Jesus did, you would crawl through broken glass to bring people to Him. No matter how broken they are.

I believed that. With everything in me. But somewhere along the way, the message changed.

I remember sitting in a service years later when that same Sunday School teacher made a joke about immigrants from the pulpit. And this time, he was not teaching children. He was leading a congregation.

People laughed. I did not. I looked around and felt like I had swallowed a stone. This was someone who once taught me that Jesus loved everyone, and now he was clapping for cruelty.

And I want to be clear. I make jokes too. I am not perfect. I get things wrong all the time. But there is a difference between laughter that lifts and laughter that wounds. And in that moment, the laughter felt like a wound.

I remember thinking, if Jesus walked in here right now, He would not laugh. He would walk out with the ones we just turned into a punchline.

That was the beginning of my disillusionment. Not with God. But with the people who claimed to speak for Him. Somewhere along the way, the church started focusing more on rules than on people. On religion instead of relationship. On required rituals instead of love.

And somewhere in all the smoke machines and sermon slides, they forgot the heart of the whole thing.

I remember praising God with a full band and a worship team waving ribbon sticks like we were training for spiritual rhythmic gymnastics. And I meant every word I sang.

I do not think the music was wrong. I just think sometimes we praise loud so we do not have to listen deep. And Jesus is often found in the silence, sitting beside the ones we are too busy performing for to notice.

Instead of crawling through glass to love the hurting, some Christians started posting memes about them. Instead of washing their feet, they mocked their pronouns. Instead of leading them to the God who saved me, they blocked the door.

That is not what my Jesus would do. People like me, people who have empathy, started being called fake Christians. Not for rejecting Jesus, but for embracing the people He died for.

I once shared a post supporting Bishop Mariann Budde after she gave a speech at the inaugural service that centered on Jesus' actual teachings. Compassion. Justice. Humility.

She talked about how faith is meant to comfort the afflicted and afflict the comfortable. She spoke about love, dignity, and lifting up the marginalized. And people lost their minds.

I posted in support of her message because honestly, I did not think there was anything controversial about it. She just said what Jesus said.

But I got called a *libtard.* A fake Christian. I received anonymous hate messages from people who claimed to love the Lord while spewing venom behind a blocked number.

And the truth is, what I said in that post was not even my opinion. It was Scripture. It was love. It was basic decency.

But apparently, those things are threatening now. I could not stop thinking about Elise's friend, a legal asylum seeker from Venezuela. Her mother had sent me texts full of fear and desperation. She told me it was not safe to go back. That their lives would be at risk. That they were seen as traitors just for leaving.

She said, "We trust God, but we cannot go back. It is war. They think we are traitors."

I told her I would pray. That I had her back. But it did not feel like enough.

Because when Jesus said love your neighbor, He did not add as long as they have the right papers.

He did not ask for citizenship. He just asked for compassion. And I have seen that kind of compassion lived out.

I saw it in my mama.

One time, a woman from church was about to have her kids taken away by CPS. Her house was in such bad shape, no one would help. They whispered behind her back, judged her, wrote her off. But not my mama.

She packed up a bucket and went over there herself. She cleaned for hours. Scrubbed things no one else would touch. Not for thanks. Not for show. Just because someone had to. That is the kind of Jesus I was raised to follow. The one who sat with the forgotten. The one who walked through the mess. The one who touched the untouchable.

And the disabled? We are often treated as the untouchables of the church. We are told we are inspiring as long as we are quiet and grateful.

We are welcome as long as we do not ask for ramps, or inclusion, or too much attention. But the moment we advocate for ourselves—, or worse, for others, we are called bitter. Divisive. Ungrateful.

I have had to fight my whole life just to be seen as capable.

And the same people who praised me for being strong were the ones who turned away when my strength looked like speaking out.

Disability is not a sin to be pitied or a problem to be fixed. It is part of how God made me.

And yet churches build stages we cannot reach. They design services we cannot access. They hold back leadership roles like we are too fragile to carry the Gospel.

But Jesus never avoided the disabled. He went to them. He listened to them. He healed some, yes, but He honored all. He did not say, get better, then follow me. He just said, come.

I remember once standing next to someone the church had whispered about for years. They were the kind of person the church always kept at arm's length.

Too different. Too complicated. Too visible in their struggle. Someone the church did not know what to do with. Not because they were lost, but because they did not fit the mold. And I hugged them on the front row of that church like the whole room was not watching.

I knew some of the people in that room thought I was compromising the Gospel. But I was not. I was living it.

Sometimes the holiest thing you can do is stay when others walk away. Sometimes it is hugging the very person the sermon was aimed at, without apology. Sometimes it is flipping the table, even if no one else is ready to stand with you.

Maybe the real question is not what would Jesus do. Maybe it is who would Jesus sit beside, and why are we not sitting there too?

Because if your faith makes you more comfortable ignoring the suffering of others, it is not faith. It is privilege dressed up in a Bible verse.

I have seen more of God in hospital rooms, messy kitchens, sideways glances across pews, and text messages from scared moms than I ever saw on a platform.

I have seen Him in people the church refuses to see. And when I talk about justice, or immigrants, or disability access, or basic human dignity, it is not because I am trying to be woke.

It is because I read the Gospels. It is because I believe Jesus was not killed for being nice. He was killed for flipping systems and loving people nobody else wanted.

The Jesus I believe in broke bread with the ones the church would vote against. He stopped mid-sermon to comfort a bleeding woman.

He invited Himself into the homes of the hated. He forgave a criminal hanging beside Him before the man even asked for it.

He was never about gatekeeping. He was always about grace. I am tired of a Christianity that talks about Jesus but does not look like Him. That hoards blessings and blames the poor.

That sings worship songs while ignoring the hungry at the door. That lifts hands in church but will not lift a finger for the hurting. So when people ask why I still believe, even after all the hurt, I tell them this. Because the God I was given healed my eyes.

And the Jesus I found later healed my heart. And I still want to be the kind of person who would crawl through glass if it meant someone else might feel seen.

If Jesus is handing out stars in heaven, I am hoping I at least get partial credit for effort. Maybe a participation trophy and a full-sugar Dr Pepper.

Not even diet, because if I have made it all the way to heaven, I better not be watching calories anymore.

And maybe one of those fancy robes in a stretchy fabric, in purple, obviously. It is only right that heaven comes in your favorite color.

And a big piece of chocolate cake with buttercream icing, because whipped is from the devil.

Because I may not have gotten it all right. But I did try to love people. Even when it cost me.

Even when they did not love me back. Even when they said I did not belong.

And I have tried to carry that into my own life. To be someone who makes room.

Even when it is lonely. Even when no one offers a seat in return.

And if you have ever loved someone who never said it back, if you have ever poured your heart into a message and stared at a one-word reply, if you have ever stayed soft in a world that keeps going quiet,

I see you. I am you. And this table has room for that ache too.

This is for the ones who never saw anyone who looked like them in the magazines and thought that meant they were not beautiful.

For the ones who learned to be quiet in every room because people looked at their skin before they listened to their words. For the ones who had to translate for their parents since they were six. For the ones who grew up on free lunch and got laughed at for their shoes.

This is for the ones who did not have a dad.

For the ones who had to clap for themselves in the stands. For the ones who learned how to shave or drive or pray by watching someone else's father. For the ones who grew up longing for a father who never showed up. For the ones who still ache on Father's Day. For the ones who still ache on Father's Day. For the ones who try to be the parent they never had.

You may not have had an earthly father, but you still have a Father. The kind who never leaves. The kind who sees you. The kind who calls you His.

This is for the ones whose mamas went to heaven too soon.

For the daughters who still reach for the phone out of habit. For the sons who wonder what kind of man they would have been if she had stayed. For the grown adults who would give anything for one more word, one more touch, one more Sunday dinner.

This is for the ones who lost a sibling.

For the ones who grieve quietly while everyone else focuses on the parents. For the ones who still talk to someone no one else remembers.

You have not been forgotten.

This is for the ones who have buried more than one parent too young.

For the ones who were told not to cry. For the ones who did everything right and still got left.

This is for the ones who are disabled.

For the ones who get stared at in parking lots. Who have to explain themselves to strangers. Who are told they are so inspiring for doing everyday things. For the ones whose bodies demand help in a world built for independence. For the ones who are tired of being managed instead of respected.

This is for the ones who are mentally ill.

For the ones who battle their own minds every single day. For the ones who take their meds and still feel off. For the ones who hear "just pray about it" and wonder if anyone understands. For the ones who have diagnoses and the ones who are still searching for answers.

You are not crazy. You are not weak. You are doing your best with a battle no one else can see. And you are not alone.

This is for the ones who are single moms.

For the ones who hold it together with drive-thru dinners and Target clearance-rack finds. For the ones who cry in the car and wipe their face before walking in.

You are doing more than anyone sees. And you are doing it beautifully.

This is for the ones who are single dads.

For the ones learning to braid hair and manage meltdowns. For the ones who work all day and still show up at bedtime with soft voices and tired hands. For the ones who carry both strength and tenderness without being told how.

You are seen. You are doing holy work too.

This is for the ones who are stepparents.

For the ones who walked in mid-story and still gave their whole heart. For the ones who show up even when they are called second. For the ones who love kids who do not always know how to love them back.

Your role is real. Your love counts. And you are not an afterthought.

This is for the ones who are part of blended families.

For the ones navigating "mine" and "yours" and "ours" with grace. For the ones who show up without needing to be front and center. For the ones building something whole out of something broken.

You are making a home, even when it is complicated.

This is for the ones who were told their sexuality made them unworthy.

For the ones who are still discovering who they are. For the ones who were punished for loving differently. For the ones who felt like they had to hide just to survive.

You are not a mistake. You are not unworthy. You are loved. Not once you change. Not if others approve. But because you were made with care and purpose.

This is for the ones who are homeless.

For the ones without a place to sleep tonight. For the ones who are called lazy when they are just trying to survive. For the ones who have been treated like a nuisance instead of a neighbor. For the ones holding cardboard signs and dignity at the same time.

I am sorry the world has been so cruel to you. I am sorry people look away instead of looking you in the eye. You are not forgotten. Even if the world passes you by, God still sees you. He still calls you His.

This is for the ones who are undocumented.

For the moms who go to work before the sun rises and hope today is not the day they are seen. For the dads who missed the birth of a child because they were crossing a border to feed them. For the teens who dream in two languages but do not feel at home in either country. For the grandmothers who whisper prayers in Spanish while folding someone else's laundry. For the ones who love this country and still live in fear of it. For the ones who are called illegal, but whose love is the most legal thing about them.

This is for the ones who are Black.

For the girl who has to be twice as smart and half as loud just to be safe. For the ones who are followed around in stores but never welcomed in the boardroom. For the ones who are tired of surviving instead of thriving.

You deserve joy. You deserve rest. You deserve to be believed and celebrated.

This is for the ones who got clean and still are not forgiven.

For the ones who are trying to rebuild but cannot outrun who they used to be. For the ones who stay sober one breath at a time.

You are not what you did. You are what you do now. And what you do now is holy.

This is for the ones who are deconstructing their faith.

For the ones who still love Jesus but are scared to say His name out loud. For the ones who lost church but not God.

You are not backsliding. You are becoming.

This is for the ones who have had an abortion.

For the ones who still cry about it sometimes, even if they believed they were doing the best they knew how at the time. For the ones who feel like they are not allowed to grieve.

Your pain is valid. Your story is yours. And your heart is still worthy of tenderness.

This is for the ones who prayed for two pink lines and got heartbreak instead.

For the ones who lost a baby before the world even knew there was one. For the ones who carried hope and buried it quietly.

Your grief is real. And your love still counts.

This is for the ones who are neurodivergent.

For the adults who were diagnosed late and finally felt seen. For the ones who have spent their lives masking. For the ones who were told they were too much when they were just being themselves.

You were never too much. You were never wrong.

This is for the ones who have been in prison.

For the ones who served their time but still carry the weight of what they did. For the ones who came out and found the world would not let them be anything but what they were.

You are more than your past. You are worthy of more than a second chance. You are still someone God can use.

This is for the ones who had to walk away from family to survive.

For the ones who chose peace over loyalty. For the ones who still cry over people they had to let go.

Grief and relief can live in the same breath. You are allowed to protect your peace.

This is for the ones who were raped or sexually abused.

For the ones who were told it was their fault. For the ones who did not say no because they were too scared to speak. For the ones who said no and were not heard. For the ones who still do not feel safe in their own skin.

You are not dirty. You are not broken. You are not alone.

This is for the ones who were touched too young by someone who should have protected them.

For the ones who still flinch when the tone shifts. For the ones who were told it did not happen, or that it was not that bad, or that it was their fault.

You deserved to be safe. You still do.

This is for the ones who survived violence or betrayal by someone they trusted.

For the ones who stayed because they were scared. For the ones who left and still question if they overreacted. For the ones rebuilding from something they never asked for.

You did not deserve what happened. And you are allowed to heal at your own pace.

This is for the ones who were beaten and then told it was love.

For the ones who hid bruises and made excuses and thought that was normal. For the ones who learned to smile through fear.

You are not hard to love. You were just loved the wrong way.

This is for the ones who live in bodies that hurt every day in ways no one can see.

For the ones who are tired of trying to prove that their pain is real. For the ones who look fine but feel broken.

Your pain is valid. Even when no one believes you.

This is for the ones who are widows and widowers.

For the ones who sleep on one side of the bed and still reach for what is not there. For the ones who wonder how to keep living when their person is gone.

Love does not end just because breath does. You carry them with you.

This is for the ones who have stood on the edge of goodbye and decided to stay anyway.

For the ones who are still here but are not sure why. For the ones who feel more numb than sad and are afraid they have stopped hoping.

You are still here. And that matters more than you know.

This is for the ones who feel stuck in the wrong life. In the wrong job. The wrong town. The wrong marriage.

For the ones who wake up wondering how they ended up here. For the ones still whispering dreams they are afraid to say out loud.

This is for the ones who are lonely.

For the ones who text first but rarely get a reply. For the ones who scroll past invitations they were never sent. For the ones who feel invisible in a crowded room.

You are not invisible to God. And you are not alone.

This is for the ones who have been the secret.

For the hidden girlfriend. The side piece. The friend with feelings. The one who was good enough to love but not proud enough to claim.

You were never meant to live in someone else's silence. You deserve to be chosen in the light.

This is for the ones who were never chosen.

For the kids always picked last. For the adults still waiting for someone to look at them and say You, you. I want you. For the ones who make everyone feel special but wonder if anyone really sees them.

You deserve to be loved without earning it.

This is for the ones battling addiction.

For the ones who are still in the thick of it. For the ones who have relapsed more times than they can count. For the ones who want to get better but do not know how.

You are not hopeless. You are still worth fighting for.

This is for the ones who have been cheated on.

For the ones who felt it in their gut before they ever saw proof. For the ones who stayed. For the ones who left. For the ones who still wonder what they could have done differently.

You were never too much. They just were not enough.

This is for the ones who are battling eating disorders.

For the girls who starved themselves trying to feel worthy. For the boys who thought muscles would make them matter. For the ones who counted every bite and still felt like they were too much. For the ones who have hated their bodies and are still trying to call them home.

You are not the size of your jeans. You are the size of your soul.

This is for the ones with learning disabilities.

For the ones who needed more time on the test but were too embarrassed to ask. For the ones who were called lazy when they were actually fighting their hardest. For the kids who dreaded being called on in class. For the adults who still carry that same shame into every meeting.

You are not stupid. You are not behind. You just learn differently, and that's allowed.

This is for the ones living paycheck to paycheck.

For the ones who know exactly how much gas is in the tank and how many meals they can make with what is left in the fridge. For the ones who smile while calculating how to say no without saying they cannot afford it. For the ones who do not splurge, not because they do not want to, but because they cannot.

You are not failing. You are surviving. And that is its own kind of miracle.

This is for the ones who are chronically ill.

For the ones who are tired every day. For the ones who miss parts of their old life that no one talks about. For the ones who are constantly asked if they are feeling better when this is just how life is now.

You are not a burden. You are living a harder life with more grace than most people will ever understand.

This is for the ones who are terminally ill.

For the ones facing a diagnosis that changed everything. For the ones grieving a future they had planned. For the ones trying to make peace while still hoping for more.

You are allowed to be scared. You are allowed to be angry. And you are still deeply loved.

This is for the ones who got labeled early.

The bad kids. The loud ones. The wild ones. The ones who could not sit still. The ADHD kids who were not trying to be disrespectful. The troublemakers who were really just overwhelmed. The ones who got sent to the office more than they got invited to birthday parties. The ones nobody believed in, but someone should have.

This is for the nerds.

For the ones who memorized dinosaur facts, who wrote fan fiction, who loved school until someone made them feel weird for it. For the ones who got picked last in gym but first for group projects. For the gamers. The comic collectors. The ones who felt more at home in libraries and online forums than in crowded lunchrooms. For the ones who were told to tone it down, grow up, be cool, when they were already brilliant just as they were.

This is for the emo kids.

For the ones who wrote poetry in the margins of their notebooks and lyrics on their arms. For the ones who wore black because it matched how they felt inside. For the ones who were called dramatic or too sensitive but were really just honest about their pain. For the ones who found family in music when they could not find it anywhere else.

This is for the ones who self-harm.

For the ones who hurt themselves in quiet corners because it felt like the only way to feel something. For the ones who covered up scars and smiled anyway. For the ones who never told anyone. And for the ones who tried to but were not taken seriously.

You are not crazy. You are not broken. You were never meant to carry that pain alone.

This is for the ones who have wanted to die.

For the ones who planned it. For the ones who came close. For the ones who wrote the note. And the ones who deleted it. For the ones who have ever wondered if the world would be better without them. This is for the ones still here, even when everything inside says not to be.

You are not weak. You are not selfish. You are not beyond saving. You are still here. And that matters more than you know.

This is for the ones I forgot.

For the ones whose stories have not been written here. Whose pain has not been named. Whose memories do not fit neatly into categories. You are not forgotten by God. He knows the ache you carry. The battles you do not speak out loud. The nights you do not think you will survive.

You are seen. You are loved. You are held. And even when the world overlooks you, even when no one says your name, even when you cannot find yourself in any of these lines, you still have a place at the table. You can find comfort and rest in His arms. Because the God who never forgets still remembers you.

And if no one ever told you these things before, I hope you hear them now in the voice of someone who would have loved you without hesitation. Someone like my mama.

She loved everyone. The loud ones. The quiet ones. The broken ones. The ones who acted out and the ones who never said a word. She would have hugged your neck, fixed you a big plate of chicken fried steak with mashed potatoes and homemade rolls, or maybe pinto beans and cornbread, depending on the day, and poured you a glass of sweet tea so full it dripped down the sides. And if you were lucky, she would have had a slice of strawberry pie waiting in the fridge too. She would have made you feel welcome before you said a single word. And if she were here, she would tell you this herself.

You matter. You are loved. You still belong. You are not beyond grace. You are not unforgivable. You are not the sum of your worst decisions. You are not forgotten. You are not too much. You are not a burden. You are not the worst thing that has been said about you. You are not the worst thing you have survived. And you are not alone.

You would have had a place at her table. And you have one at mine.

CHAPTER THIRTEEN

She's Not Fragile Like a Flower, She's Fragile Like a Bomb

There are things I still wrestle with. I still question my worth when I walk into a room. I still catch myself apologizing for taking up space. I still hear voices from my past when I look in the mirror.

Voices that told me to shrink, to be quiet, to make myself smaller in every way.

I still struggle not to be the peacemaker when peace has already been shattered. And I still have to remind myself, daily, that scars are not shame. They are survival.

That is why I had the words inked into my skin. A lyric from P!nk's "All I Know So Far." Just one line, tucked low on my leg like a secret I can carry with me always:

> *They can't tell you to change who you are. Stay unfiltered and loud. You'll be proud of that skin full of scars.*

But if I could, I would tattoo the whole damn song. A song that says what I could not always say out loud. Because I am still trying to believe it.

But she, she lives like it is already true. My daughter has always felt things big. She does not cry quietly. She storms.

She does not hold things in. She lets them rip, raw and real, across the room.

There are days it is hard. There are moments I have watched her fall apart in ways I recognize too well. Rage that masks fear. Silence that masks sadness.

Frustration that makes it hard to even breathe. But she is growing. She is fire and fight and feeling. She is boundaries I did not know how to set. She is truth I did not know how to speak.

She is the courage I prayed would come in the next generation, and there it is, living in my house, slamming doors and hugging hard.

She reminds me so much of my mama. That fierce love. That do-not-mess-with-my-people fire. That deep-down softness wrapped in sharp edges.

She has got her fire, and Lord help the world when she learns how to channel it.

Over time, I have come to believe Elise's fire is not a flaw.

It is her calling. And that means my job is not to tame it. It is to help her channel it.

Elise is smart. She is funny. She is capable of great compassion. And sometimes, she struggles. She wrestles with impulse, frustration, and intensity. There are days she feels too big for her own skin.

There are days she does not like me.

Days she pulls away, rolls her eyes, shuts the door a little harder than necessary.

Days where I feel like I am standing on the outside of her world, knocking instead of being invited in.

And if I am honest, it still hurts.

Not in a fragile way, but in a deep, familiar one.

The kind that whispers, "You are too much," even when I know better now.

But somewhere in the middle of that ache, I remember...

I did the same thing to my mama.

I pushed back.

I got sharp.

I acted like I did not need the very person I needed the most.

And she loved me anyway.

Not perfectly. Not always gently. But faithfully.

So now, when Elise looks at me like I am the problem,

I do my best to stand where my mama once stood.

Steady.

Present.

Not chasing her approval, but not withdrawing my love either.

Because this is not rejection.

It is becoming.

Sometimes she comes back five minutes later like nothing happened.

Leans into me like she didn't just push me away.

And I let her. Every time.

But that does not make her broken. Because what the world calls too much, I call miraculous.

Add this after: Because what she was really saying was this: do not protect me from the truth just to keep things gentle.

She reminds me of Peter.

The kind of heart that speaks before it thinks.

The kind that loves big and reacts fast and sometimes gets it wrong in the middle of trying to get it right.

He was the one who said the bold thing, did the impulsive thing, felt everything out loud.

And still, he was chosen.

Still, he was trusted.

Still, he was called to lead.

Not because he was steady.

But because he was willing.

When the storm is out, run in the rain.

But that does not make her broken. Because what the world calls too much, I call miraculous.

She is the best and hardest parts of everyone who came before her.

She is my second chance to raise a girl who believes she is good even when she feels messy.

She is not the quiet kind of strong. She is the storm. The shift. The spark.

I used to think strength meant silence. But watching her has changed that.

My mama would have been so proud.

She would have bragged about her to every person who made her wait too long in line.

She would have watched her blaze through life with that soft half smile she used when something hit her heart just right.

She would have seen herself in Elise. And she would have seen something more too.

I want everything for her. I want her to love Jesus in a way that feels safe and kind. To help others with hands that do not hurt.

To love someone who sees her completely and chooses her anyway.

To live free of the shame I carried like a second skin. To walk away from cycles that tried to pass themselves down like a family recipe. I want her to be happy.

And more than that, I want her to be good. Not quiet good. Not rule-following good. But good like kind. Good like brave. Good like I will love you anyway kind of good.

She is becoming all of that. She will be strong without first being broken. She is already braver than I ever knew how to be at her age. And she is strong in a way that heals me.

Because watching her grow into someone who feels her feelings and fights for her space and stands up even when she is shaking is like watching a piece of me rise up and finally breathe.

And maybe the most powerful thing of all, she is doing what my mama and I never could.

She is breaking cycles we did not even have the words for.

She is carrying the same fire, but instead of being consumed by it, she is learning how to light the way.

I know it is not easy to feel everything so big. I see how fast she goes from laughter to tears. How her anger shows up first, even when what she really feels is fear or disappointment or hurt.

And I want her to know, that is not a flaw. It is a fire. And fire, when channeled, makes warmth and light. But when ignored, it burns through everything good.

So here is what I hope for her. When the heat rises, breathe first. When her voice shakes, use it anyway, but use it with love. When she wants to throw something, write something instead.

When she feels like she is too much, come to me. And when the world tries to tame her, I hope she remembers I never wanted her tamed.

I just want her whole. And someday, hopefully long, long from now, I know she will learn how to live without me.

It breaks my heart to say it, but I need to believe it. Because that is the truest proof I ever did my job right. If she can carry this fire without burning down.

She was never meant to be small. She was made to take up space, to love out loud, to make the world uncomfortable in all the right ways. But I want her to do it without losing herself to the fire. And then there are moments when she already shows me she is on her way. One afternoon, she glanced at my phone and saw a message that upset me.

It was not cruel, just dismissive. Cold enough to sting. Soft enough to second-guess.

She looked at me and asked softly, "Are you okay?"

I told her I was just having a hard day, but I was trying to be kind anyway. That sometimes when people are hurting, they hurt others too, and I was doing my best to give grace even when it was not easy.

She sat quietly for a moment. Then she said something that stopped me in my tracks.

"When I am mean and someone comes back with kindness," she said, "it makes me sad. So I wish you would just tell me to stop."

I told her, "But when I do that, you usually get mad."

And she looked me straight in the eye and said, "I would rather be mad than sad."

That cracked something open in me.

Because what she was really saying was this: do not protect me from the truth just to keep things gentle.

When the storm is out, run in the rain.

Put your sword down. Dive right into the pain.

Those are her words now. And mine too. I want to be better, even if it stings.

She was asking for accountability. She was saying, do not let me get away with hurting people, even if I push back. Do not leave me alone in my guilt.

Show me how to grow. And I heard her. I've got you, baby girl.

Because for so long, I confused silence with kindness. I thought grace meant shrinking.

But she reminded me that real love tells the truth, even when it is uncomfortable. Especially when it is uncomfortable.

She is becoming the kind of girl who asks to be called higher. And I am becoming the kind of woman who will not let her stay small.

She is a world changer. Not someday. Now. One hard conversation, one unfiltered truth, one brave act of love at a time. And I get to be the one who witnesses it.

What a holy, ordinary gift that is.

People think fragility means weakness. That it is soft and delicate and cannot hold weight.

But she is not fragile like that. She is not fragile like a flower. She is fragile like a bomb. Full of force. Full of feeling.

And if you do not handle her with care, not caution, but respect, she will shake the ground beneath your feet. Not to destroy. But to change something. Because that is what she does.

She breaks silence. She moves rooms. She does not wilt. She detonates. And someday, when she learns how to use that power with purpose, the world better make room.

CHAPTER FOURTEEN

My Greatest Story

I do not have much to leave behind. No heirlooms. No handwritten journals. No secret treasures tucked away in a chest at the end of the bed. All I have is this. My voice. My story. And I will be honest. It hurts to put it all in writing. To lay it bare.

But I am doing it for you. So you will know what is really inside.

Not just the memories I have shared out loud, but the ones I carried quiet. The ones I did not always know how to say.

The truth of who I am and who you are to me. I only have one thing left from my mama.

Her Bible.

The pages are soft from years of turning. Some are underlined in fading blue ink, and the corners are bent where she marked her place. And it still smells like her.

Sand and Sable perfume. The kind that clings to memory long after it has left the room.

When I miss her most, I open that Bible. Not for the verses, but for the places her hands touched.

I trace her handwriting like I am reaching for her. It is how I hold her now. And when I think about what I want to leave you, it is this. These words. These pages.

I open that Bible, and I hope you will be able to do the same with this. That when you need me, you will turn these pages and feel me right there with you.

I wonder sometimes what she would think of the way I raised you. If she would be proud. If she would see her fire in your eyes. But I think she would. Because I have loved you the way she loved me. Fiercely. Protectively. With everything I had.

For James

My firstborn. My strong and steady one. You are a hard worker, kind and considerate, the one who is always looking out for others. My protector. My peace.

You were the first person to ever call me Mom. The first heartbeat that changed mine forever.

You made me a mother, and nothing in my life has ever mattered more than that.

From the beginning, you carried something quiet and steady in you. Even when you were little, there was a calmness, a thoughtfulness, a sense of responsibility that most grown men never master.

You were never just a kid who needed raising. You were a soul who came here already carrying light.

And I saw it. I still do.

But you were still my little boy.

The one who ran through life a little too fast, tearing his jeans and laughing like it didn't matter.

The one who didn't always realize how good he was, even when everyone else could see it.

You have always been strong. Not loud or showy, but the kind of strong people feel when you walk into the room.

You are steady. Reliable. You do not waver when life gets hard.

You hold the line for the people you love. You show up, even when you are tired. And you have done that for me more times than I can count.

You have helped carry this family in ways most people will never fully know.

But hear me when I say this now.

You were never supposed to carry me.

I am grateful for the ways you showed up. I will always be grateful.

But that was never your weight to hold.

You do not owe me strength.

You do not owe this family your shoulders.

You get to be held too.

I hope you build a life that does not require you to be the strong one all the time.

I hope you find people who show up for you the way you have always shown up for everyone else.

I hope you learn that love is not something you have to earn by being dependable or steady or needed.

You are worthy of it just because of who you are.

You are a good man, James.

Not just because of what you have done for us, but because of who you are at your core.

I hope you let people see the parts of you that do not always have it together.

The parts that are tired. The parts that need. The parts that want to be chosen too.

You deserve a life where you are not just the one holding everything together.

You deserve to be held too.

And there is something else I want you to know, even if you have never said it out loud.

You are not going to be overlooked.

You are not going to be too quiet to be chosen.

The right woman will see you. Not just what you do for people, but who you are when you are just being yourself.

She will see your steadiness, your loyalty, your heart, and she will not take it for granted.

You will not have to prove your worth to her.

You will not have to carry her just to keep her.

She will meet you with the same kind of love you have always given.

The kind that stays. The kind that shows up. The kind that feels like peace.

And when that day comes, I hope you let yourself receive it.

Not with caution. Not with doubt.

But with the same open heart you have always given to everyone else.

And I know there are days you feel like you should have it all figured out by now.

Like everyone else is moving forward and you are still standing still.

But hear me clearly. You are not behind.

You are building your life in a way that actually lasts. Quietly. Steadily. Without pretending to be something you are not.

There is no timeline you have to catch up to. No race you are losing.

You are working. You are showing up. You are becoming.

And that matters more than having all the answers right now.

You do not have to rush into a life just to prove you are moving forward.

The right path will meet you when you are ready for it.

And no matter where you go or what you decide, there is no version of your life where you are not already enough to me.

You took care of your siblings when I could not. You watched out for me when I was the one falling apart.

You have been my protector, my helper, my quiet strength. And you never once asked for credit.

You are a hard worker. You give your best even when no one is watching.

You are kind. Not just in small ways, but in the way you treat people. In the way you notice what needs to be done. In the way you love without needing to be asked.

You are a protector by nature, and it is not just something you do. It is who you are. You protect with your presence. With your heart. With the way you look out for people like it is your calling, even when no one sees it.

You are also the one who makes me feel loved when I feel like I am all alone in the world. The one who watches over me when I was supposed to be the adult.

You help me out of the car without being asked. You hold my hand when I cannot see and the ground is uneven. You always know. And you always act.

You have never waited to be told. You just do what love does.

You called me the other night on your way home from work. You never call at that time, so when I saw your name pop up, my heart dropped. I just knew something had happened. But all you said was, "I ripped my last pair of jeans."

I laughed with relief, and because of course you did. You have been splitting pants since kindergarten. I lost count of how many times I brought fresh uniform pants to the school. Somehow, even now, those tiny moments still carry a hundred memories.

You apologized for bothering me. Said you didn't want me to have to get up early and go buy more jeans before your shift. But what you do not know is that I do not see that as a responsibility. I see it as a privilege. Still being able to show up for you, even in small ways, feels like a gift.

You tower over me now. You make me feel safe. But in that moment, all I could see was my little baby James. The one who used to run full speed into life and tear his pants wide open on the way.

I know I have not always gotten it right.

I have been tired. I have been overwhelmed.

I have made mistakes and let my own pain spill out when I should have been softer. But I never stopped loving you. Not for one second.

I hope this world never hardens you.

I hope you find people who love you the way you have loved us. With loyalty and quiet fierceness.

I hope you give yourself the same grace you have given others.

I hope you never feel like you have to carry the whole world on your back to be enough. You already are.

I hope you fall in love with someone who sees your heart and does not take advantage of it. Someone who respects your strength but also lets you rest. Someone who listens when you speak and holds your hand when you are quiet.

You deserve softness. You deserve peace. You deserve to be chosen.

I do not know how I got lucky enough to have you for a son.

You are my anchor. My safe place. My reminder that I did at least one thing right in this world.

When things got hard, you were the one who steadied me. Who held things together when everything else was falling apart. Who loved us through it all with more maturity than some adults ever manage.

You have always deserved more. More rest. More peace. More people recognizing just how rare you are.

I hope when you think of me, you do not just remember the hard seasons or how much I leaned on you.

I hope you remember that I saw you. That I knew you. That I loved you in a way words will never fully hold.

And when I am not here anymore, I hope you always know where to find me. In the quiet. In your strength. In the way you love others.

I will still be with you. Always.

You are not just my son. You are one of the finest men I have ever known.

You are one of the greatest gifts my life ever gave me.

And even though your height towers over me now, you will always be my Sweet Baby James.

I love you forever, Mom

For Eli

My brilliant boy. My question asker. My thinker. You keep me on my toes and light up every room with curiosity.
My genius, and you know it.

You were never ordinary. Not from the beginning. You asked questions most kids never think to ask. You saw things most people never notice. And you have always been two steps ahead of the rest of us.

You are not just smart. You are the kind of brilliant that can change the world. Because you do not just know things. You understand them. And then you figure out how to fix what is broken, not just with your brain, but with your heart.

You do not just want to be good at something. You want to be the best. You want the trophy. The title. The win. And you chase it with everything you have.

But I know the truth behind that too. You do not just love attention. You need to know you matter. You need to feel seen.

And sometimes, when I tell you how proud I am, you think I am just saying it. Like I am trying to make you feel better.

But I am not.

Eli, you really are a winner. Even on the days you do not win.

And even more than that, it is okay if you are not always the best. It is okay if someone else comes in first. It is okay to stumble.

You are still good. You are still important. And you are still mine.

I know that when you lose, or when you are afraid you might, you do not always show how hard that hits you. Except when it is just us. In the car. That is when you let it out.

That is when I see your heart wide open.

And I need you to know I never take that for granted. You feel things deeply, even when you try to hide it. You care more than you will ever admit.

And that does not make you weak. That makes you powerful.

Because the best minds in the world are the ones that can think sharply and love fiercely. And you were born with both.

I will never forget the day we saw the sick homeless man in McDonald's. It was storming outside. He had his head down on the table and looked like he was in pain. The employees wanted him to leave. They said he was chasing customers away.

He was not loud. He was not bothering anyone. He was just sick.

And when I asked if I should buy him food, you did not just say yes. You said, "Get him a Sprite. It will help his stomach and there are free refills." But then you went even further.

"Get him a gift card," you said, "so he can come back tomorrow if he feels better. And if the workers try to kick him out, they will have to let him stay because he will be a paying customer."

You did not just show kindness. You thought ahead. You protected his dignity. You tried to make sure he would be safe not just for that moment, but for tomorrow too.

That is how your mind works. That is the kind of heart you have. And that is the kind of man I hope you grow into.

You do not just notice injustice. You quietly undo it.

But I know that sometimes you get overwhelmed. Sometimes you feel like you will never be enough. Sometimes you push harder. And sometimes, you give up too soon.

So here is what I want you to carry with you, even when I am not around to remind you.

You are enough. Not when you win. Not when you get everything right. Not when people clap for you. You are enough right now, just as you are. Even when it is messy. Even when it is hard.

I hope you never lose your questions. I hope you never stop chasing big dreams. But I also hope you learn to rest. To let go when you need to. To know the difference between pressure and purpose.

I hope you fall in love one day with someone who sees every part of you. Someone who laughs at your jokes, marvels at your mind, and knows how deep your heart really goes.

I hope you get the family you already dream about. The wife. The kids. The home filled with noise and love and ideas. And I hope they get the best of you.

Because the best of you is world changing.

You do not have to be the loudest to make a difference. You just have to be you.

Smart. Curious. Brave. And kind in a way that most people never even learn.

You are not just my son. You are one of the brightest, most remarkable souls I have ever known. And if I could choose you a thousand times over, I would.

I love you forever, Mom

For Elise

My warrior girl. My mirror. My softest place. When the world feels too loud or too heavy, I hope you will remember how deeply you are loved. Even when you think no one sees it, I do. I always have. I always will.

You are my warrior girl. From the very beginning, you came into the world with fire in your spirit and strength in your bones.

You are bold. You are brave, even though you swear you are not. And you are yours, completely and unapologetically.

You have always done things your own way. You do not follow the crowd. You do not quiet down just to make other people comfortable.

You walk through the world with power and presence, and sometimes that power feels like a lot to carry.

But I need you to know something. It is never too much for me. And neither are you. You are not hard to love. You are not a problem to fix. You are not a burden.

You are a miracle. You are a gift. You are my daughter. And I have never once stopped being grateful for that.

There have been moments when the world did not understand you. When people expected you to be smaller, quieter, more agreeable.

But I have seen you clearly from the beginning.

I know how fiercely you feel things. I know how loyal your love is. I know how often you hold your pain inside because you do not want to show anyone that you are hurting.

But baby, you do not have to hide from me.

I can handle your fire. I can hold your softness. You are safe with me. Always.

You were almost four years old the day you looked up at me and said, "Girls never give up. Boys may give up, but us girls never give up even if we can't stand up to pee."

You had no idea I was waiting to find out if my tumor was cancer. You were too little to understand what was happening, but I believe with my whole heart that God was speaking through you. Those words carried me through one of the scariest moments of my life.

And now, as you grow, I know there are moments when you feel like you are the one people give up on. When friends do not stay. When the people you trust most stop showing up. When you feel like your heart is too big or your feelings are too deep or your personality is just too much for this world.

But baby, that fire in you has never left. You are still the girl who said we do not give up.

And even when your own voice shakes, you are the one who teaches me how to keep going.

You and your brothers are the reason I never gave up either. Even when it would have been easier. Even when I wanted to disappear. I would have, if not for you. Loving you three has always been the reason I fight to stay.

I know it is not easy being a girl in this world, especially one who knows her worth and refuses to settle.

But I hope you never dim your light to make someone else feel brighter. I hope you never shrink to fit a space that was not made for you. I hope you never silence your voice to keep someone else's peace.

And I hope you never confuse someone's discomfort with your power as a sign that you need to change.

You are powerful. You are beautiful. You are allowed to take up space.

There will be days when you feel like no one gets you. Days when the world feels too loud and your thoughts feel too big.

And on those days, I hope you hear my voice in the back of your mind, reminding you that you are loved. That you are not alone. That you are worth fighting for, even when you feel tired of fighting.

You are the girl who can walk through fire and come out stronger. You are the girl who will not just break cycles but build something better in their place. You are the girl who can be both lightning and shelter.

And I see every part of you.

I see the way you love fiercely, even when it is hard. I see the way you care deeply, even when you pretend not to. I see the way you watch people closely, trying to figure out who is safe and who will stay.

One time, you made a list of all the things you love about me.

You said I am kind. That I always put you first. That I make sacrifices. That I am funny, even if it is "Facebook mom humor."

You said you love my food. My strength. The way I always stand up for people. And you even pointed out that I know the difference between "your" and "you're."

That list made me laugh and cry at the same time. Because that is who you are. Fierce and funny, observant and loyal. You see everything. You feel everything. And somehow you still love with your whole heart.

So let me be clear.

I will always stay.

There is nothing you could ever do that would make me stop loving you. Nothing too messy. Nothing too loud. Nothing too hard. Nothing too much.

You are exactly who you are meant to be.

And when you grow into the woman you are becoming, I hope you keep choosing yourself. I hope you walk away from anything that makes you doubt your worth. I hope you say no when you mean it and yes only when it feels right in your bones.

I hope you love someone who sees every part of you and never asks you to tone it down. Someone who loves your fire and knows how to tend it instead of trying to put it out. Someone who knows that your strength is not a threat. It is a treasure.

And I hope you still love yourself. Fully. Honestly. Proudly.

You have so much ahead of you.

And I know there will be days when you question everything. But do not ever question this.

You were wanted. You were chosen. You were loved more than words can ever hold. And you always will be.

You are not just my daughter. You are one of the fiercest, most extraordinary souls I have ever known.

And even if you were not mine, I would still want to know you. But I am so glad you are mine.

If I could choose you a thousand times over, I would.

I love you forever, Mom

For James, Eli, and Elise,

And then, a note for the three of you together, because you will always belong to each other, and to me.

There is no greater gift I have ever been given than the three of you. You are so different. So entirely your own people.

But you came from the same place. The same heart. Mine.

And no matter how many years pass, or how far life takes you, you will always belong to each other.

I hope you know how much I have loved being your mom. Even on the hardest days. Even in the chaos and exhaustion and worry. It has been the greatest honor of my life.

I know I have not been perfect. But I hope you always knew that I was trying. That I showed up with everything I had, even when I had very little left.

You saved me in more ways than you will ever know. You gave me a reason to keep fighting when I did not think I had any strength left. You brought laughter into rooms that had held silence for too long. You reminded me that love is louder than pain and that hope is stronger than fear.

I want you to know that I am proud of each of you. Not for your accomplishments or your grades or your trophies. But for who you are when no one is looking. For the way you keep showing up. For the way you love. For the way you carry pieces of me forward, even when you do not realize it.

I hope you chase the life you want with everything you have. I hope you let yourselves dream. I hope you work hard. I hope you rest when you need to. I hope you find people who love you well. And I hope you never forget to be those people for someone else.

You do not have to be perfect. You do not have to get everything right. You just have to keep going. Keep being kind. Keep being brave. Keep being yours.

And when life is heavy or confusing or just plain hard, I hope you press into Jesus. Not just the version people try to twist into something mean or small. But the Jesus who healed people, loved outcasts, fed the hungry, and wept with his friends. The Jesus who saw people others ignored. The Jesus who still sees you. Talk to Him. Trust Him. Let Him hold what you cannot.

I hope that even though there is an age gap between you, you never let it divide you. I hope you never grow apart. Because one day, I will not be here to hold the three of you together. So I hope you will hold each other.

I hope you will lean on one another when you feel like you cannot stand. I hope you will pick up the phone and check on each other. I hope you will laugh about the good times and talk through the hard ones. I hope you will sit beside each other at hospital beds and birthday parties and kitchen tables.

You are each other's history. You are each other's roots. No one else will ever understand what it was like to grow up the way you did. No one else will carry the same pieces of me that you do. So when you miss me, when you need me, find each other. That is where I will be.

I remember how Eli would crawl into Elise's bed just to talk when she could not fall asleep, like his voice was enough to calm the storm. That is the kind of love I hope you keep giving each other.

I hope one day, when you have families of your own, you remember the love that held this one together. Not because it was perfect. But because it was real. Because it was fierce. Because it never let go.

If anyone ever tries to hurt you, I hope you remember whose daughter and sons you are. My mama would have fought for me. And I will fight for you twice as hard.

You three are the best thing I ever did. You are the proudest thing I ever offered the world. And if I could choose you again, if I had the chance to go back and do it all over, I would choose you. Every time.

You are not just my children. You are my heart walking around outside my body. And you always will be.

With all the love I ever had, Mom

You three are my greatest story. If you ever forget, read it again. I will be right there, even if I am not.

CHAPTER FIFTEEN

The Strength She Left In Me

I see her in flashes now. In the way I pull food from the oven and silently hope it tastes like hers. In the protective way I love my children, even when I am exhausted. In the songs I sing when no one is listening. In the ache I carry that never really goes away.

She is still here. She has been gone for years now, and still, some days I reach for the phone to call her. Still, I whisper things out loud as if she might be near enough to hear. Still, I look for her in the sky when the sun hits just right or when my heart is too heavy to carry alone.

Grief never really leaves. It just grows quieter. It stops shouting and starts humming in the background. And if you love someone deeply enough, you learn to live with the hum.

Grief is love with nowhere to go. It is also the price of love, and I would pay it over and over again if it meant I got to have her as my mama.

She gave me so much while she was here. And the truth is, she still is. She is giving me strength even now. The kind that held her up when she should have fallen apart. The kind that carried me when I could not carry myself.

I did not know how much of her I would need until she was no longer here to give it to me. And still, I find pieces of her inside me. When I speak up. When I fight back. When I show up for someone who is hurting. When I love my kids with a kind of fury that says nothing will ever come for you without going through me first.

She is the reason I never gave up. Not all the way. Because even when I wanted to lie down and disappear, I could still hear her voice. Saying no. Saying stand up. Saying not yet.

The world did not love her gently, but she loved gently anyway. The world did not give her peace, so she created it inside our home. She was not given tenderness, so she poured it into me. And now, I carry it all.

I carry the legacy of a woman who should have broken but did not. I carry the weight of a life she did not get to finish. I carry the ache of questions she never got to answer. I carry the fight, the faith, the fire. I carry the strength she left in me.

I wish I could say that loving this fiercely means I have always been loved in return. But the truth is, even now, I am often met with silence. I speak with tenderness and people look away. I reach out and they shrink back. I stay soft anyway. Because that is the strength she left in me too.

I have spent most of my life carrying extra weight, not just on my body but in my spirit. Trauma settled into my skin. Grief lived in my appetite. And for a long time, I believed that being small would make me worthy. But I did not lose weight to become someone else. I lost it to find the parts of me that got buried under the heaviness of everything I was never meant to carry.

It is something my mama never could quite do. And maybe that is why I needed to. Not just for my body, but for my breath. For my mind. For my freedom. For the daughter she never got to watch live lighter.

I used to think I had to wait until everything was tied up with a bow before I could tell my story. But maybe the truth is, it was never meant to have a perfect ending. Because life does not wrap up neatly. Loss still aches. Love still stretches. And I am still becoming.

So this is not a conclusion. It is a continuation. Of her strength. Of my voice. Of every broken, beautiful thing I am still trying to carry forward. And if you are still unfinished too, you are not alone.

I hope she is proud of me. I hope she sees the parts of her I tried to carry forward, the way I fought for my kids and for others who could not fight for themselves. The way I told the truth. The way I stayed soft, even when the world gave me every reason to harden. That is who I yearn to be.

And even on the days when I feel like my race is already run, when the doubt creeps in and I wonder if my life was wasted, I remind myself I am not done. I still have more to do. More differences to make. More stories to tell. Until I overcome every obstacle that tried to silence me so that someone else will pick up this book and believe they can survive too.

I believe God allowed me to go through every one of these struggles, not because He abandoned me, but because He trusted me. He knew I would use them to show others that mountains can be moved. That pain can preach. That scars can speak.

And I may run slow, but I will not stop. I will walk. I will crawl if I have to. But I will keep going. Because I know who I came from. And I know what she left in me.

Her grave says Tammy Denise Webb Dixon. Born November 5, 1958. In heaven November 18, 2006. Gone but not forgotten. I picked those words. And now, I have to live them. I have to make them true.

So I picture her now, standing in heaven. No more pain in her body. No more weight on her shoulders. Just light, and love, and peace. I hope she is smiling when she sees me. And I hope she hears the words she always deserved.

Well done, good and faithful servant. You finished the race you were given. And even though it was cut too short, your legacy still echoes. You poured yourself out in love. And your love is still here.

The fight did not die with my mama. It lives in me now. In the way I speak. In the way I stay. In the way I rise.

She did not just teach me how to love. She showed me how to do it when it is hard. When it costs you. When no one claps or says thank you. When the world misunderstands you or moves on without noticing.

My mama did not just teach me these words. She was these words. She lived them when no one was watching. She lived them when it hurt. She lived them when the world gave her every reason not to. And I have spent my whole life trying to live that same way.

Do It Anyway

I grew up with the words often attributed to Mother Teresa, "Do it anyway."

People will misunderstand you. Be kind anyway.

They'll question you. Do what's right anyway.

Not everyone will be honest with you. Tell the truth anyway.

Some will overlook what you give. Give anyway.

What you build may not last. Build it anyway.

Some days it won't feel like enough. Give anyway.

The world will take more than it gives. Love anyway.

People love to say, "Don't cross oceans for people who wouldn't cross a puddle for you."

No. Do it.

Do cross oceans for people.

Love people, all people.

No conditions attached, no wondering whether or not they're worthy.

Cross oceans, climb mountains.

Life and love aren't about what you gain, it's about what you give.

In the end, this was never between you and them. It's always been between you and God.

I hope I make her proud. And when my children look back on my life, I hope they can say the same about me.

That's who my mama was.

I've always been proud to be hers.

EPILOGUE

A Letter to My Younger Self

Dear Little Me,

I know you feel like you take up too much space. Like you were born with too many needs and not enough worth.

I wish I could sit beside you in those cafeteria moments. The playground ones. The hospital beds. I would not tell you to toughen up. I would tell you that you are enough, just like that.

I know you are wondering why people leave. Why some people do not look you in the eye. Why some boys laugh instead of love. And why it hurts so much to keep trying to be chosen. I know you are wondering if daddies really are supposed to stay. Because the songs said they never go away. But sometimes they do. And I am so sorry you had to learn that too soon.

But you have a mama like most people will never get to experience. And her love will hold you together when everything else falls apart.

I wish you knew you were already chosen. I wish you knew that one day, you would raise children who see you as safe. That you would write a book that makes strangers feel known. That you would walk through hell burned but not consumed. That you would survive what should have undone you.

You will not always feel broken. You will not always believe you are too much and still not enough. One day you will understand that silence does not mean you are unworthy. Some people will not know how to hold what you carry. They will pull away. They will not answer. But you will learn to keep loving anyway. You will learn to stay soft anyway. And that will be your superpower.

And even though you roll your eyes when your mama tells you you are special, even though you think she does not get it, or that her words are just things moms say, hold on to them. She was right. They are all true.

You were never made to fit in. God made you to always stand out. One day, you will look back and realize your softness was never a weakness. Your story was never shameful. And your voice was never too loud.

You are going to make it. And you are going to help others make it too.

Love, Me
Still healing. Still going. Still becoming.

The Woman My Mama Knew I'd Become

I've been called:
GARBAGE.
FAT.
UGLY.
DEFORMED.
EVEN RETARDED. (I hate that word)
But here's what they didn't count on:
Every insult taught me something they didn't mean to.
How to speak up.
How to survive.
If they hadn't tried to tear me down, I wouldn't have learned how to stand up.
Not just for me but for others.
I don't yearn to be liked anymore.
I'd rather make a difference.
I want to help people feel seen, heard, and strong in the places they were once made to feel ashamed.
So if you ever tried to break me -
Thank you.
You taught me how to fight.
And I'm not afraid of you anymore.
I WILL FULFILL MY PURPOSE.
NO MATTER THE COST.

www.ingramcontent.com/pod-product-compliance
Lightning Source LLC
LaVergne TN
LVHW010947110826
845149LV00015B/3249

* 9 7 9 8 9 9 5 9 1 2 4 0 8 *